The Family Whistle

To: Howie and ELLEN GERSHMAN

The Family Whistle

✦

A Holocaust Memoir of Loss and Survival

Simon Eichel

with Lee S. Kessler

iUniverse, Inc.
New York Lincoln Shanghai

The Family Whistle
A Holocaust Memoir of Loss and Survival

iUniverse books may be ordered through booksellers or by contacting:

iUniverse
2021 Pine Lake Road, Suite 100
Lincoln, NE 68512
www.iuniverse.com
1-800-Authors (1-800-288-4677)

ISBN-13: 978-0-595-36136-6 (pbk)
ISBN-13: 978-0-595-80577-8 (ebk)
ISBN-10: 0-595-36136-6 (pbk)
ISBN-10: 0-595-80577-9 (ebk)

Printed in the United States of America

Written on the fortieth anniversary of my father's death: June 30, 2000.

I dedicate *The Family Whistle* to my mother, whom I knew for such a short time and remember very little. I was only fifteen years old when she perished in Auschwitz.

I dedicate *The Family Whistle* to my brother Moniek, whom I knew an even shorter time and remember even less. He was only eleven years old when he perished in Auschwitz.

I dedicate *The Family Whistle* to my sister Lisa, who, in my mind, is a princess not only in beauty, poise, and dignity, but also in love, warmth, and compassion. She perished in Auschwitz.

I dedicate *The Family Whistle* to my brother Josel, whom we all admired for his guts and jovial attitude that made the darkest moments in our life look bearable and hopeful.

I dedicate *The Family Whistle* to my brother Salo, who was always considered the fragile and weak one, but was the most resourceful; he always managed to bring home some "bacon" when plain bread was a luxury.

I dedicate *The Family Whistle* to my father, who helped me survive; whose love and encouragement provided the drive needed to survive, progress, and succeed; and whose wisdom always was—and is—a guiding beacon in the labyrinth of my life.

Note: Why is it that when I write these words I feel like crying?

Contents

Preface

By David Scrase

Sixty years after the end of World War II and the carnage of the killing centers, memoirs by survivors continue to appear. Such memoirs encompass so many varied experiences, and demonstrate so much resourcefulness, so much courage, and such determination on the part of the survivors that their readers are continually astonished at what seems to be almost unlimited fortitude. In addition to the sterling human qualities of strength, courage, and resolve, there was also (inevitably) luck and happy coincidence. Whether one was able to survive depended on so many factors, not least of which were geography and chronology. Whereas flight from the Nazis and from the gradually worsening situation for the Jews in Germany was largely to the west before the war began, everything changed in September 1939 when Germany invaded Poland. First Polish Jews and then, rapidly, all other Jews in Europe found it next to impossible to escape westward. Most European Jews, caught between the Germans to the west and the Soviet Union to their east after the defeat of Poland, chose to remain where they were, and assumed, much as the German Jews had assumed in the 1930s, that things would change.

Some, soon acutely aware of their rapidly worsening situation, looked to the stratagems of hiding, or passing as Christians. They could do so only if they had the material means necessary, only if their physical characteristics allowed them to blend in with the Gentile community, or if their linguistic background did not betray them. (Yiddish as a first language was hard to disguise.) Often they could survive only if they had Gentile friends willing to risk their lives to help.

There were also those who resolved to escape from the Germans by fleeing east to try their luck in the Soviet Union or Asia. Circumstance cast Simon Eichel into this group. He is also one among those survivors who made their way as part of a family group who stuck together through thick and thin, and whose mutual aid and support enabled them to live. He is also one among those survivors who came of age during their ordeal. Such teenagers accordingly grew up very fast, and attained a degree of maturity so quickly that adolescence was missed.

In this regard, Mr. Eichel's story is not just a memoir, which records events and adventures recollected and set down more or less chronologically. The players in such memoirs are often somewhat flat and one-dimensional. *The Family Whistle* is rather a true autobiography, which shows the growth and development of the central character, the maturation of a young boy into a mature grown man. The process and the personal growth are effectively conveyed despite the sober and unemotional style of the narrative. The anger, fear, desperation, and grim thoughts that mark so many survivor accounts are absent here, or muted. There is an acceptance of, and a constant adaptation to, the current circumstances. Hence the picture of life on the periphery of the gulag is less an indictment of the system and more a portrayal of conditions in Siberia during a desperate time. It is not only an effective account of one man's fight to live, but also an illuminating description of the events of World War II as they unfolded in Central Europe and in the far reaches of the Soviet Union, beyond the military action and beyond the horrors in the occupied territory. Mr. Eichel's story is a different tale, a complementary tale, an effective and vivid story that grips us and leaves us the richer for having read it. It is a sober, unemotional, and objective tale that is rich in quiet dignity.

David Scrase is the director of the Center for Holocaust Studies at the University of Vermont. He is the editor, along with Wolfgang Mieder, of four books of collected Holocaust essays including *The Holocaust: Personal Accounts.*

Prologue

A lifetime can be made up of many lifetimes, each one in a different world, in a different language, with different criteria for living, in war or in peace. If it were up to me, I probably would never have gone far from my father's house. But of the many choices life presented to me, staying at home was not one of them.

I recently thought about these many lifetimes while I was grocery shopping with my wife. Mary and I were married in 1948 in Ulm, Germany. Today we live in Westchester County, New York. Our local supermarket is large and clean, well-stocked and well-lit; just a normal supermarket. But anyone who has been hungry can marvel a little at a normal American supermarket. Anyone who has known scarcity can view such gaudy abundance with a little bewilderment. As I looked back, these lives I've led seemed far away, yet at the same time ever-present, like the internal organs of the body. You don't think much about them, but they're inside you, an inseparable part of who you are.

Mary was in another aisle of the supermarket and I wanted to find her, so I whistled the family whistle. It came to my lips as effortlessly as her name, as effortless as breath. Hearing the notes of the whistle echo across the wide aisles, I thought of how much of my life has been affected by this fragment of a song.

The family whistle was originated when I was still a baby by my oldest brother Salo. He would occasionally come home from a date or party after ten o'clock, when the landlord had already bolted the iron gate of our apartment building on Karl Strasse. There was a bell at the gate that rang in the landlord's apartment but he did not take it kindly if someone woke him, especially some reveling teenager like Salo. To yell up to our second-floor apartment from the outside of the court-yard wall would also wake up the landlord and the neighbors too. So Salo decided to whistle up a short, happy melody as a signal, then my sister or my mother would go down and let him in. He whistled a line from a song he sang as a German Boy Scout, "*Horch, was kommt von draußen 'rein.*" Roughly translated, it means "Hear what's coming in." A good choice, I guess, since *he* was coming in.

This subsequently became the family whistle that we used whenever we got separated on the street, in the park, or any other public place. Eventually we could even distinguish who was whistling. It was something I took for granted as a child and I suppose, at times, I must have wondered why others didn't have their own family whistle.

To reminisce like I did that day in the supermarket is unusual for me. I don't normally dwell on the past. Why should I? Life is very rich and full in the present. But it was on my mind because I had recently uncovered, in some storage boxes in my house, two notebooks. I wrote them in 1946 while in the Displaced Persons Camp in Ulm, shortly before I met Mary. The ink has faded on the brittle paper and the cursive handwriting, though unmistakably mine, is not like my handwriting today. Reading the words written in German by the young man who was me brought the memories back, across the worlds and gulfs of language.

I've always written about my life, just to get things off my chest. I never really thought about it as anything more than that. Looking back, I guess you could see it as a kind of compensation for the youth I didn't have; all the passionate discourse that school friends have together as they grow up and figure out their lives. I have written a lot that I've been forced, by circumstances, to destroy. Believe me, it's no great loss to world literature. Yet these two notebooks survived, pulled out of a dusty cardboard box. I have no reason to destroy them now. Just the opposite. This book is derived from them.

I am a Holocaust survivor, and I want to do my part—however small—to make sure that people remember the atrocities caused by prejudice and the suffering caused by war. I could say I was unlucky to be born Jewish in Poland in 1924, the year Hitler wrote *Mein Kampf,* and that fate was cruel to tear me out by the roots. But it was also fate that delivered me newborn to my father's house. To him and to two of my brothers, I owe my many lifetimes. It was also fate—so often accompanied by the whistle of a short, happy melody—that saw me through hardship and struggle across three continents.

1

Invasion

In 1939 I was fifteen; old enough to be aware of the apprehension running all throughout our city, yet too young to really understand that these "politics" could significantly affect my life.

After World War I, Upper Silesia was divided in half. Our city, which was once in Germany, was now in Poland, five kilometers east of the border. Once called Königshütte, it was now called Chorzow. Our street, where the teenage Salo had whistled up at night, was renamed Ulica Mieleckiego. The population of Chorzow was about 110,000, many of whom still thought of themselves as German.

We spoke German in our home. Though Simon was my Jewish name from birth, I was called Siegfried, a name given to me by my sister Lisa and brother Salo, who were both schooled in Germany and were socially oriented that way. Their social set felt that German culture was more refined and they looked down on most Poles. I did not even know that my name was Simon until I went to school where the Polish teachers saw it on my forms and favored it over Siegfried, which was too German for their taste. Lisa, Salo, and my second oldest brother Josel surely were not too happy when our city became part of Poland. But they were much older than me. I felt myself to be Polish, even with the German culture of my family.

By August, the drone of anxiety had grown loud in the shops, markets, and streets of Chorzow. Germany had already taken Austria and part of Czechoslovakia, and there were signs that Poland would be next. Hitler had demanded the "northern corridor" of Poland containing Danzig so that he could link Germany with Prussia. He had also demanded the return of the Polish portion of Upper Silesia.

The optimists of Chorzow noted that England and France had signed a pact to protect Poland from invasion. England and France behind us! Surely that would mean a world war if Hitler invaded Poland, they said, and surely he's not that crazy. The pessimists only had to point to Austria and Czechoslovakia.

My father owned a tailor shop and a clothing store in Chorzow. He remembered World War I military tactics where entrenched armies fought across well-fortified lines, battling for years and leaving the poisoned land looking worse than the moon. Though skeptical of all the dire predictions, he nevertheless felt the border was a little too close for comfort. Around the middle of August, we packed our suitcases for a temporary visit and took the trolley to the city of Sosnowiec, a city fifteen kilometers to the east that had a large orthodox Jewish population, among whom I felt alien. My parents, my younger brother Moniek, and I stayed there with my mother's parents on Targowa Street. Salo and Josel stayed at home to watch the store. If trouble did arise, they could take the trolley to Sosnowiec to join us. My sister Lisa and her family (husband Alex and five-year-old son Felix) were also staying in Sosnowiec with one of Alex's brothers.

Sosnowiec was in Poland. It was not part of Upper Silesia. The anti-Semites in our city called it the Polish Palestine. In our city or any of the other Upper Silesian cities, you hardly ever saw a Jew with a long beard. In Sosnowiec, it seemed like most of them had some kind of beard. I didn't like Sosnowiec. However, I did like my Uncle Jicryk, his wife Yochia, who was my mother's sister, and their family who lived there. Jicryk was less than six feet tall and a bit on the husky side. He had the dark stubble of a beard on his face. Always joking around, he was generally a jovial person. Whenever we visited Sosnowiec, we always went to his salami store on Ulica Dekerta. He had all kinds of salamis and a few tables and chairs where you could sit and eat and enjoy a glass of tea. He would always greet me with "The Yekke is here!" which is what Polish Jews called Germans.

"Which of my delicious salamis would you like?"

He knew I'd answer "frankfurters." I always told him his frankfurters were the best I ever ate.

Salo and Josel went into center Chorzow each morning to see what was happening. Then they went to the store to conduct business as usual. Thursday, August 31 began the same way. This time, as they walked, they noticed very few people on the streets and a conspicuous absence of police. The trolleys were not operating. Then they heard what sounded like shooting from the west. That did it. Instead of going to the store, they went to see our Uncle Yankel, my father's older brother, who lived only a few blocks away from us. Salo and Josel could not persuade Uncle Yankel that it was best to go.

"Me and my family will not leave," he said. "Where will we go? If the Germans should come, what can happen? As bad as they are, they are not animals. They are just as human as we are."

Salo and Josel returned to our apartment and packed. They took clothes, some food, and, for protection, my father's big tailor scissors. Then they walked all the way to Sosnowiec, arriving at my grandmother's apartment late in the afternoon. We were all there, including Jicryk, Yochia, and their family. At night, some of us slept at her apartment. Salo and Josel slept across the hallway at a neighbor's, who had fled the city and left the keys with Aunt Yochia.

At three o'clock in the morning, we were awakened by a loud fist pounding on the door. Alex, Lisa's husband, was there with the whole mob of his brothers. The oldest, Moisze, was a reserve officer in the Polish army. He told us Germany had invaded and their army was close by. The Polish army had already retreated from the city and declared total mobilization. Moisze and his brothers decided to catch up and join the army. He suggested that Salo and Josel come too. Salo and Josel were both over twenty-one years old. For them, failure to report to the army could be construed by the Polish authorities as desertion. They looked to my father and he sadly nodded his agreement that they should go. My mother, crying, hurried to prepare some food for them to bring. Being just an immature kid, I was excited by this midnight call to action and wished I could join them. I understood nothing about war. To the weeping of the women, the young men hurried away in the night.

The next day, Friday, September 1, at about 1:30 on a sunny afternoon, I was standing with my mother on Targowa Street in front of Grandma's building. It was about 100 feet from the intersection with Mondziejowska Street, the main thoroughfare. I noticed a commotion amid the crowd on Mondziejowska and it seemed like everyone was staring in the same direction up the street.

"I'm going to see what's going on there," I said and headed toward the corner.

"Be careful," my mother called. "Don't walk too far from the house."

At the corner, I noticed that everybody was looking down Mondziejowska, but the street curved and I couldn't see anything. So I crossed to the other side to get a better view. I kept on walking down Mondziejowska, craning my neck, without realizing that I could no longer see my grandma's building or my mother. I was about to turn back when I heard loud gunshots up ahead and then the rattling of a huge tank, followed by more shooting. People began running away. The middle of the street, which only a moment ago was full of people, was now clearing fast. I saw a tank approaching me. People vanished into the nearest buildings.

At first, I started to sprint toward Targowa, but I realized that to get back I'd have to cross the street, and the tank was shooting down the middle of it. I decided to take cover inside the nearest building. By now, the iron gates of the street doors all along Mondziejowska were being slammed shut. The grinding of the tank grew louder behind me as I barely managed to squeeze into a building just before someone pulled the gate closed. There were about a dozen people who had taken cover in the interior walkway. I was the only kid. We were gripped by a stunned silence.

Through the bars in the iron gate, we saw the first tank rumbling past the building. Then German soldiers walking close by, looking up and pointing their rifles at the roof tops of the buildings on the opposite side of the street. There continued to be sporadic gunfire. Many more tanks passed and many more soldiers.

We stayed there, staring silently through the bars, for more than an hour watching the endless stream of the German army. I cursed the curiosity that led me to stray from my grandma's door. There was no one in our frightened nest to comfort me. The sporadic gunfire continued at the front of the column as it moved away out of our hearing. The soldiers and equipment in a long stream continued to go by. I longed for the end of the column to pass, so I could rush back to my grandma's place. I would run so fast, I'd be just a blur. But then a couple of German soldiers stopped at our gate and knocked it with their rifle butts. They saw us cowering at the back of the walkway. They shouted "*alle raus*! (Everybody out)" and motioned us into the street with their rifles. We went out and they herded us, a silent throng appearing out of every building, down Mondziejowska Street. As we passed Targowa, I strained to see some sign of my mother, but I couldn't. I hoped she was all right as I trudged obediently along.

They brought us to the railroad plaza, only a few blocks away. There were hundreds of people in the crowd and the Germans were dividing them into two groups, shouting "*Juden hier*! (Jews here)" and motioned to the group on the left. The Gentiles were herded into the group on the right side of the plaza. There was great confusion at first because a lot of Poles did not understand German. Then several lines formed that each lead up to a soldier. When I came to the front, an officer looked at me and barked "*Jude?*"

I don't know what it was that guided my reply to him. I was not calculating or scheming. I was not even consciously thinking. I was in shock, afraid, and unaware that a surging tide of world history had just scoured Mondziejowska Street in Sosnowiec and I was separated from my family. My grandma's apartment on Targowa Street, really so close, may as well have been a thousand kilometers away.

When the officer asked me if I was a Jew, I replied, without hesitating, in crisp German, "*Ich bin von Königshütte* (I am from Königshütte)." Königshütte is the German name of our city. He asked my name. I answered, "Siegfried Eichel." The name Siegfried was on my school ID card, which I showed him.

"What are you doing here alone?"

"I am here with my parents visiting friends."

"Go back to your parents," he said. "Tell them that tomorrow morning the trolleys will be operating again and you can go back to Königshütte."

He motioned to a soldier to let me through. "Let him pass!" was called behind me as I walked out of the crowd, lightheaded and free, on to Mondziejowska Street.

Walking back on the empty street, I heard a few shots fired in the distance. I began to hurry. When I finally came to my grandmother's building, I found the big iron gate was locked. The family whistle came to my lips. It echoed up the empty stairwell behind the gate. After a moment, I heard footsteps in the stairwell and my mother's voice calling "Siegfried? Siegfried, thank God!" She wept and thanked God as she hurried down to the gate. "Thank God you're back!" She reached to open the gate, but a look of panic came over her face. The gate was padlocked. She tugged at the unyielding lock and said, "Wait here. I'll get the landlord."

She turned to go back up the staircase. However, at that moment, I heard the sound of an engine and shooting coming close on Targowa Street. I saw a German soldier driving a motorcycle with a sidecar. Another soldier was in the sidecar with a gun. I also noticed (all of this must have happened in the fraction of an instant) that the door in the building across the street was partially open. There was a body lying in the doorway.

"Mother!" I shouted. "I'm going across the street."

She turned around in horror, holding both hands on her face.

"Siegfried!"

There was more shooting, and the motorcycle was getting closer. I bolted across the street to the doorway. I stepped over the body of the dead man, avoiding the puddle of blood near his head. I went into the hallway.

This was the first time I saw a real dead body. Up until now I had seen them only in the American cowboy movies. But this was not like that. I ran into the hallway and vaulted up the stairway to the first floor. I knocked at the first apartment door, but no one answered. I went knocking from door to door, but no one answered. The same thing happened on the second floor and the third. I was ready to go down again when I heard a baby crying behind one of the doors. I returned to it and continued to knock forcefully. After a minute or so, the door opened slightly. I saw a young woman.

I said in Polish, "I am visiting my grandmother across the street, but I can't get back in because the gate is locked. Can I stay here for a while?"

I could see that she was scared. She did not answer, but she turned her head slightly toward a man standing behind her. He was middle-aged, had a small beard, and was wearing a "capele" or yarmulke on his head. He was Jewish.

He asked me in Polish, "What is the name of your grandmother?"

"Hampel," I said.

"What is your name, and where do you live?" he asked, this time in Yiddish.

"Simon Eichel. And I live in Chorzow," I replied in Yiddish. I could see he was suspicious, maybe because my Yiddish had a German accent. Also my appearance was not a familiar one in Sosnowiec. I was wearing my high school uniform; a navy blue jacket with silver buttons and cap with a shiny visor.

"What is your father's name?"

"Avrum," I said his Jewish name, even though everyone always called him Adolf. The baby began crying even louder, so he pulled me inside and locked the door behind me. We were now standing in a hallway with a few closed doors and an opening to the dining room and living room. There was food on the dining room table. A middle-aged woman sat there with the fretting baby in her arms. The man saw me looking in the direction of the dining room and asked, in a more kindly tone, "Would you like to eat something?"

"Thank you, but I'm not hungry," I answered. Eating was the last thing on my mind. Here I found myself in an apartment, not so different from the one I lived in, with a family, only not my family. In this near familiarity, the extraordinary events of the past few hours played again in my mind. The soldiers and shooting…the fear…the pounding heart in my chest…the tortured face of my mother behind the gate…the horrible sight of a dead man lying in a dark pool of blood. And the worst thing was the uncertainty—just when I had been so close to her—of what would happen next. I wanted to cry, but I was too numb and overcome.

The man walked me toward the door at the end of the corridor and showed me into a small bedroom. He whispered something to the young woman. (I guess it was his daughter.)

I heard him say, "Stay and watch him."

She came in and spoke to me in Polish, "Sit down," pointing to a chair at a table near the window. I was very glad to sit down.

"Would you like something to eat? We have plenty of food, and I will gladly bring you something."

"Thank you, but I just couldn't eat now."

She sat down on the bed, looking at me. The minutes of silence that followed would have been embarrassing to me under normal circumstances, but I was still numb.

"What school do you go to?" she asked.

"I just finished the second-grade level in the *gymnasium* (high school) in Chorzow." School and home, how far away they seemed.

"Is this your *gymnasium* uniform?"

"Yes," I answered.

After a moment, she left the room, probably to report about the uniform. I could understand their concern. It did look somewhat military. And they were frightened about what was happening, just like I was. After a few moments, she came back and we resumed our silence. I was just too worried to carry on a conversation. I stared blankly out the window, which looked out on a small courtyard. Now and then, the sound of shooting echoed over the town. When would this end?

After an hour or so, I noticed a rope dangling outside the window that was being gradually lowered from the roof. As I pointed this out to the young woman, she leaned over to look. Then we saw a pair of boots and then legs coming down. She screamed. There was a man standing on the ledge of the window holding on to the rope.

She cried "Yakob! Yakob!"

She hauled the window open and helped the man into the room. I sat dumbfounded. The girl's father rushed into the room and embraced the man, who was around fifty years old. Speaking in Yiddish, he told us what had happened to him. He too was on the street at the time the shooting started. He originally wanted to run to their house, but, when he saw the German soldiers coming down the street, he ran into the building next door and stood in the hallway for a while. Afraid that the Germans might see him, he walked up the stairs to the top floor and then managed to get onto the roof. Then it occurred to him that, if the Germans should find him on the roof, they might shoot him. He crossed over to the roof of their building but found the roof door locked. Looking around, he saw a rope near the chimney, probably left there by the chimney cleaners. He tied the rope to the chimney and, knowing that their apartment was immediately below, lowered himself on the rope to the window ledge.

I was amazed. He was not a young man and certainly did not look like he had the strength or daring to do such a dangerous thing. But he did it.

As darkness descended, closing this horrifying day, the random shooting stopped. The town fell silent. My adopted family—I never even asked their names—frequently scanned the street from their front windows for some sign of normalcy. But the streets remained empty. After some discussion, they decided it was not safe to go out of the apartment. They showed me where the bathroom was and told me I could use the bed in the little room where I had been sitting. I slept fitfully.

Early in the morning, around seven o'clock, we looked out of the window and saw some people on the street. My adopted family thought it would be safe for me to go. I thanked them and went cautiously down the stairs. Descending to the street door, I saw that the dead man had been taken away. The pool of his blood had also been rinsed away, but the floor was still stained.

In the morning sunshine, people moved through the streets in a gloom. I crossed quickly to my grandma's building and found the gate was open.

When I walked into my grandma's apartment, my mother screamed, "He is here!"

She cried and hugged me so hard that it almost hurt. They all thought I was dead, shot by the Germans. Yesterday when I ran away from the locked gate of the building, my mother heard shots and was sure that I had been killed. They had said Kaddish for me, the Jewish prayer for the dead.

My father went out later in the morning and determined that the trolley was indeed operating, as the German officer had told me. He decided we should go back home, though Lisa, Alex, and their son remained in Sosnowiec.

When we got back to Chorzow, we saw a lot of Nazi flags flying from apartment house windows; red banners with black swastikas everywhere. I wondered where they had gotten so many flags so quickly. I credited German efficiency.

Life in the city seemed normal except the police were in German uniforms and no one spoke Polish on the street any more. Most stores were open. What was even more surprising to me was when I met school friends who greeted me with "Heil Hitler." These were the same guys who, only a week before, had portrayed themselves as staunch Polish patriots. Only one of my classmates, Hanke, greeted me as before, "Hallo Siegfried!" I liked Hanke. Once in the classroom of an anti-Semitic teacher, we discussed Jews in Poland. I was the only Jew in the class. Hanke, quite to my surprise, stood with me in the discussion.

That first day back in Chorzow, Hanke and I walked together for a while. It felt good for me to tell him what had happened to me in Sosnowiec. After one of our classmates passed us with a Heil Hitler salute with his rigid arm outstretched, Hanke turned to me.

"We were wasting time debating Jews in Poland at school," he said. "And the Polish Parliament was wasting time in their kosher debate, too. They should have been talking about how to stop the German Fifth Column from infiltrating and corrupting our country."

I'll always have respect for Hanke. He had the guts to think for himself and not go along with the mob. The German Fifth Column he referred to was a gang of agitators who came in to join with the local Nazi sympathizers to spy and try to corrupt local officials. They provoked unrest, instigated anti-government rallies, and spread rumors.

The Polish Parliament debate he referred to was a well-publicized deliberation on the important issue of the kosher food laws as they applied to the slaughter of poultry. It was a great concern to many members of the Polish Parliament that the kosher method of killing chickens was unnecessarily cruel.

2

Josel's Job

A few days after we returned, England and France declared war on Germany. Weary, old Chorzow was renamed, once again, Königshütte.

If you ignored the Nazi banners and the "Heil Hitlers," life in our city seemed back to normal. There were no air raids or sirens, no shooting. One would hardly know there was a war going on. We sat at lunch that day wondering when we might get word from Salo and Josel. The Polish army had not engaged the Germans yet and were probably still in retreat. It might be a month or more, my father guessed, before we'd get word. As we ate, we heard footsteps coming up the stairs in our building and then a knock on the door. In walked Salo and Josel.

"Are we late for lunch?" Josel asked.

After the hugging and greeting, my mother set plates for them and we heard their story. The night they left us in Sosnowiec, they walked east with Alex and his brothers and reached the town of Mondziejow, where Alex had cousins. They learned the Polish army had already retreated still farther east. The band of young men got some sleep in Mondziejow, then went on the next morning, walking east.

But they never reached the Polish army. Instead, the advancing German army reached them. They were rounded up with hundreds of other people on the road. Here too, the Germans separated the Jews. Salo had joined the Jewish group, but Josel grabbed him out.

Josel was blond and did not look Jewish. He spoke flawless German, but the biggest thing in his favor was his monumental, audacious poise. He was always completely unflappable.

He walked up to the nearest German soldier and said, "I am from Königshütte, Upper Silesia. My name is Josef Eichel, and this is my brother."

The guard promptly herded them into the non-Jewish group. They were kept under guard overnight and were released in the morning. They never knew what

12

happened to the Jewish group. Then, as we had done, they rode the trolley back home.

That's Josel. Again and again in our family, Josel would do something to astound or confound us. In the end, all we could do was shrug and say, "That's Josel." He had an expression of his own devising, "schmoy-boy." In all the languages spoken in our home, this meant nothing in any of them. He would use it as if to say, "It's no big deal." He always casually tossed it off, perhaps with a flip of the hand, a tilt of the head, and a roll of the eyes. "Schmoy-boy."

After a week, we learned that Warsaw had fallen. The western half of Poland was now occupied by Germany and the eastern half by the Soviet Union. My father and Salo went back to work in the store. Josel, a barber by trade, had lost his job because the Jewish owner of the shop where he worked had fled the city.

Then a postcard came from the city headquarters of the Nazi party addressed to Josel. It informed him that there was a job available for him in a barbershop, giving an address not far away. It even stated the salary, which wasn't bad. They instructed him to contact the owner as soon as possible.

We were the only Jews in our building. If we had any hope of making it through the war, it was by keeping our heads down and staying out of trouble. This Nazi invitation was certainly trouble. My father was upset. He showed Josel the postcard.

"Oh good," said Josel.

"Good?" my father yelled. "This is good?"

"Sure," said Josel. "It's a job."

"It's from the Nazi party! Josel, how did the Nazis get your name?"

"Last week, I went along with Horst to the party headquarters. We registered for a job," he replied.

It was easy, like a walk in the park. Horst, the son of our neighbor in the building, was a good guy and a friend of both Josel and me. Under the new regime, registering for a job in this way was the only legal avenue to get work. It was not premeditated on Josel's part, but Horst was going to register, so Josel simply went along with him. My father stared at Josel for a long moment of pure disbelief.

"And you didn't tell them you're Jewish?" he finally yelled.

"They didn't ask," Josel replied calmly.

"No wonder they didn't ask!" my father screamed. "What Jew is going to walk into the Nazi party headquarters and register for a job?" He threw his arms up in complete exasperation.

It was a crisis; as if Josel had formally invited the Nazis to come inspect our home. With all of the real dangers of life for Jews in troubled times, Josel had to go out and invent a new one of unimaginable magnitude.

My mother cried and shouted, "How could you do this?"

My father sat stunned. Turning the problem over in his mind, he was unable to really comprehend Josel's action. If he reported to work and later on was discovered to be Jewish, there was no telling what would happen to him and to our entire family. We had lived there my whole life, and everyone knew we were Jewish. We never hid it. On the other hand, if Josel did not report to work, it would definitely look suspicious, he would have to explain why, and again, there was no telling what would happen.

"Oh, how could you do this?" my mother wailed.

Salo took Josel aside and asked him the same thing.

Josel began, "Schmoy-boy, this is…"

"No," Salo interrupted. "Don't give me that. What on earth were you thinking?"

"I don't know why everybody is making such a big deal. Horst was going. I went with him. I had no problem." He shrugged. "I'll go to work, and I'll have no problems. If I don't go now, they will ask questions. It's better if I go."

Salo looked Josel in the eye and saw that he was not afraid, and agreed that he should report for work. Salo sat my mother down and soothed her, and he convinced my father that Josel should go. My father would always be baffled, unable to comprehend the image of a Jew strolling in to Nazi party headquarters for a job; unable to comprehend how his own son could do it.

But then, that's Josel.

3

Deportation

After his first day of work, Josel came home quite happy, telling us that the boss was a nice guy and was very happy with Josel's work and the way he handled his customers. He noted that some of the customers were officers of the gestapo, who had their headquarters nearby.

A few days later, he came home bragging. "I was shaving a gestapo officer, and he was telling me that the worst problem is the *"verfluchte Juden* (cursed Jews)." Every country should get rid of them," Josel smiled, mimicking a gruff voice. "I was shaving his neck, and it occurred to me how easy it would be to just…" Josel mimed slitting the throat with a graceful pirouette, then looked down in mock horror at the mistake. "Oops!" he laughed.

Moniek and I were doubled over with laughter. Moniek fell off his chair and rolled laughing on the floor. My father wasn't laughing.

"Josel, it's your neck I'm worried about. And ours."

Things were fine for a couple of weeks, then came a public notification from the German authorities. They informed the Jewish Community Council that all male Jews ages eighteen to fifty must report at 9:00 AM on October 16 to the Turnhalle (gymnasium) for work on farms and factories. The notification required each man to bring along food for two days and work clothes for thirty days.

Salo and Josel were in that age bracket. For them to have to go was not really a problem. We assumed this was a just temporary requirement. But what about Josel's job? What would he tell his boss? To confess that he was Jewish now was, of course, out of the question. On the other hand, if he did not show up at the Turnhalle, the gestapo would surely track him down. And imagine them finding him in their own barbershop! My parents were in panic. We all were terrified, except Josel of course. Schmoy-boy!

The next day, he came home from work, smiling.

"Everything's fine," he said. "I told my boss I received a notice to report for labor duty and will not be able to work for him. He told me he knows some important people and that he would have no problem in getting me excused. I told him I don't want to be excused. I want to go and serve my fatherland." Josel's face mimicked the starry-eyed patriotism of his boss and, imitating his voice, said, "Josef, you're doing the right thing. I am proud of you."

Proud of his dance through this minefield, Josel then smiled at my parents.

"I told you not to worry," he said.

My parents breathed a sigh of relief, saying in Yiddish "Thank God for that." And so ended that crisis. We expected Salo and Josel would return soon, riding on the trolley as they had done before. They went away without tears. Each had a new short coat that my father bought for them, the kind worn by common laborers in our city. It looked very odd to me to see my brothers with these coats; it just wasn't right.

A few days later, the only synagogue in the city was burned down to the ground. The authorities took no pains to conceal the fact it was arson. The police stood idly by while festive looters carried out prayer books and other religious articles, waving and playing with them as if they were toys.

That same week, the authorities announced that no one was allowed to listen to foreign radio stations and all Jews must turn over their radios to the police. I remembered how Salo, just a few days before he left, was turning the radio dial when he came upon a station playing Jewish songs. Never before had we heard Jewish songs or Yiddish-speaking announcers; a pleasant surprise. It was coming from Lvov, a city in eastern Poland now occupied by the Soviet Union. A few months before, Molotov and von Ribbentrop, with Stalin looking on, had signed the German-Soviet Non-Aggression Pact. The Jews in Lvov had to deal with the Soviets, but they were free of Nazi persecution. They could have their own radio program.

Our landlord came up to our apartment and asked if we were aware of the new decree. He spoke German. Before the war, less than two months earlier, this patriot of Poland would speak only Polish. But whatever spirit he had was broken, like his country.

"Yes," my father told him. "I'm aware. I'll take care of it first thing tomorrow morning."

"Well," the landlord said apologetically, "I'm here because we landlords have been instructed to check all our Jewish tenants. I know you have a radio. So, if you'll give it to me now, I'll take care of it for you."

With his head down, my father hesitated a moment. Then he looked up and invited the landlord to take the radio. He even thanked him. Hastening to be away from this embarrassing scene, the landlord gathered the large radio up in his arms and went out. The table where the radio sat looked empty now, only some dust where it had been. My mother hastened to get a dust rag.

The mood in the Jewish community had become depressed and fearful. Any fond hopes that we might be left in peace were vanishing in the autumn breeze that blew the red banners hanging from the buildings. A few days after the radio was taken away, some town officials came to my father's store. They informed him that they had appointed a German to manage the store. My father, who had built his business up from nothing, was instructed to obey the new manager and not interfere. Again, he acquiesced to the authorities. Perhaps, he hoped, this new manager would not be hard to live with.

But he never really got the chance to find out. Exactly two weeks after Josel and Salo left, the Germans increased the age range. This time, they called up Jewish men between fifteen and sixty. Again, they were to report to the Turnhalle to be assigned to work on farms and factories. I was fifteen, and my father was fifty-eight years old. This meant my mother and younger brother Moniek, who was eleven, would remain. My father was worried about leaving them alone. We had heard nothing from Salo and Josel, so we didn't know when they'd be back.

My father went to consult with his brother Yankel. He was over sixty years of age and had only one son, Izik, who was seventeen. He told my father he would not allow his son to go. He would tell the authorities that Izik was ill.

My father consulted with other Jews in our city and most of them felt that there was no choice but to report to work as directed. There was another Jewish family that had the same problem as us. The man was a tailor and occasionally did some work for my father. He had a family of three children with one son who was subject to report. My father took me along when he went to visit them. Judging from the apartment they lived in, they were rather poor compared to us. I was surprised when the man addressed my father with great deference as "*Pan* (sir) Eichel."

"I am going to take my family and go back to my parents who live in Mondziejow," he said in Yiddish.

He had come to Chorzow only a few years earlier.

"Isn't that dangerous?" my father asked. "After all, the Germans are in Mondziejow, too."

"I don't care," he said. "If I have to hide, I will. But I will not leave my family."

On our way home, I asked, "Father, what will we do?"

He considered his answer for a long moment as we walked. "We are not in the same class as these people," he explained. "We cannot go into hiding and jeopardize the whole family. We can't live that way."

After a great deal of discussion between my parents, it was decided my father and I would go. My mother and Moniek would stay in the city as long as they could. Hopefully, Salo and Josel would return soon. However, it was left for my mother to decide if and when she wanted to go stay with her mother in Sosnowiec. For the most part, we thought of this as a temporary inconvenience that we had to endure as best we could.

In keeping with the German decree, my father bought himself a short laborer's coat, as he had for Salo and Josel when they went away. To see my father in such clothes was even more jarring for me than seeing my brothers in them.

In life today, in America, as I write this, clothes do not have the meaning that they did in Europe when I was a boy. Today, you might see a man in work clothes, such as blue jeans. You do not know if he is a ditch digger or company president. But when I was a boy, things were more formal. One's clothes told all about one's economic station in life and in the community, values, and standards. The world treated you the way it saw you. So, to see my brothers and my father wearing clothes that were so far beneath them was much more than an offense to my standard of style. It was an offense to their true identity.

At 9:00 AM on October 30, my father and I went to the Turnhalle. I wore my long custom-made school coat. My father could not see me wearing work clothes. My father took along a small knapsack with some clothes, sandwiches, and a bottle of milk for the trip. I had my knapsack. On the way out, our next-door neighbor, (Horst's father) gave us some butter, which was very hard to come by. We were cheered by this friendly gesture. He assured us this was only a temporary measure because Germany was at war.

When we arrived at the Turnhalle, we were "asked" to sign a statement that we came voluntarily for work. Nobody dared to refuse. We then had to line up and stand at attention until everyone signed the papers. There were about 200 people and about twenty gestapo officers. As we stood at attention, I saw Uncle Yankel enter the hall. He told one of the gestapo officers, "My son is very sick and cannot come."

The officer directed him to the table where he spoke to another officer. After a while, I saw Uncle Yankel leaving the hall. I admired my uncle's efforts to get his son Izik excused, even though we knew he was not sick.

After standing at attention for about a half hour, we were told to march in step around the hall while the gestapo shouted commands, sometimes kicking those who were not in step. After an hour or so of drilling, we marched onto the street escorted by the gestapo officers.

As we marched on the street, we saw my mother and Moniek walking along the sidewalk waving to us. I saw the tears in my mother's eyes and the desperation on her face.

Moniek scowled as he was pulled along behind my mother.

"Ah!" my father blurted. "I forgot the *letzgelt* for Moniek! How could I?" he bitterly chastised himself.

Whenever my father went away on business trips, he would give Moniek and me a going-away present that we called *letzgelt*. It was a small amount of money, usually about twenty groszen. But this time he forgot. A little boy of eleven does not know about the hatreds and conquests that tear the world into destruction. He only wonders why, when he's been good, he doesn't get his *letzgelt*. He knows it's not fair. We marched away with my father in anguish at his mistake.

We marched about seven kilometers to the freight railroad yard on the outskirts of the city of Katowice. There we boarded a freight train, sixty people jammed into each car. My father held me close to make sure we didn't get separated and were able to board the same freight car. As we entered, we noticed two pails on the left, one with a cover and the other filled with water. He anticipated that the covered pail was to serve as a toilet, so my father pulled me toward the opposite end of the car. When they closed and bolted the door from the outside, the car was packed full. There were a few small openings of about six by twelve inches on each side of the car to let in fresh air. The train lurched violently, and people fell over each other as we started to move east into Poland. It stopped intermittently, and it seemed as if more freight cars were being added.

We traveled for two days. No one could sleep since there was not enough room for everyone to lie down. The best thing we could do was sit down with our legs bent in front. I managed to doze off from time to time. It was hard not to scream sometimes, being so confined. The sandwiches and milk we brought were like a luxury in that dusty, bumping freight car. When I ate, I thought again of the kindness of our neighbor who gave us butter.

The covered pail was indeed used as a toilet, and I was glad we were on the opposite end of the car. I hoped I would not have to use the toilet, but, even though I tried to hold it in, eventually I had to go. Worse than the stench was my embarrassment at using that pail while people were close around me.

The train stopped a few times, but we were not allowed to get off. A person standing near the pail was ordered to empty it in the field nearby, wash it, and also fill up the water pail from the water pump.

On the second day, the train stopped in a grass field, a few kilometers past the village of Nisko. Knees aching, we climbed down into the late afternoon sunlight.

We were told to line up facing the train. Soldiers shoved people into lines. As hard as my father tried to hold onto me, we got separated when a soldier grabbed me and told me to go to the left end of the line. Another soldier pushed my father in the other direction. There must have been at least a thousand people lined up in five long rows, our knapsacks at our feet. Forty or fifty soldiers and officers were facing us. Five machine guns set up in the freight cars, pointing toward us. One of the officers began to address us in German, shouting to be heard.

"I have orders to shoot all of you! However, I will not do it if you give your money and jewelry to the collecting soldiers."

Soldiers with cloth sacks were starting to collect from each end of the lines. I was numb with shock. How could this be happening? I wondered if they were going to take our money, but shoot us anyway. I wished I could be standing with my father. When the soldier came to me, I gave him all the money I had, fifty marks, and the gold watch my parents had given me for my bar mitzvah.

When the systematic theft was completed, the same officer began shouting again. "As I promised, we will let you go. I will whistle three times. On the first whistle, you will get your knapsacks. On the second whistle, you will start running toward the woods behind you. On the third whistle, we will shoot anyone who is still in this field."

On the first shrill whistle blast I put my knapsack on, heart pounding. I stared down the line trying to see the officer with the whistle so I could anticipate the next signal. On the second blast, I turned and ran as fast as I could, dodging around the slower men, bent for the woods, 500 feet away. The ground was uneven and it was slow going, like running in deep sand. In my native city environment, I could be around the corner and gone like lightning, but here I seemed so slow. I tried to spot my father, but it was chaos.

After thirty seconds or so, the third whistle sounded. Like an arrow, it pierced the pounding sound of my breath as I pulled air into my lungs. The machine guns began firing.

In terror, I dropped my knapsack to run faster. I was one of the closest to the woods, and I was still 400 feet away. Around me, people were falling. I didn't know if they were shot or tripped. It suddenly occurred to me that dropping the knapsack was a mistake, since it provided some small protection from getting shot in the back.

To my own astonishment, I started praying aloud in Hebrew as I ran, "*Shema Yisroael, Adonoi Elohenu, Adonoi Echod* (Hear, Oh Israel, God is Almighty, God is One)." It was the only prayer I could remember from my rather casual study of Judaism.

I reached the woods alive, exhausted, and I collapsed out of breath against a tree trunk. I looked back and saw people were still running. The machine guns were still firing. Some were still falling, others struggling back up to their feet. My eyes clawed the terrible scene for any sign of my father. There was none; only terrified men, struggling toward me.

Then the shooting stopped. Silence echoed, and I heard voices crying and calling out. In the field, the stragglers still labored toward the woods. Perhaps all the men who fell got up again. Robbed and run off, but not murdered, amazed to be alive. In the woods all around me, dazed men walked aimlessly back and forth, shouting names, friends and loved ones separated. Some wept openly.

In the ensuing moments, fear washed over me anew and then sheer panic. What would I do without my father? Where would I go? I suddenly felt much younger than my years and helpless as an infant.

Without realizing it, I had been screaming, "Father! Father!" but it was useless. Everyone else was screaming names too. I decided to try the family whistle. But my heart was pounding and my lips were dry. No sound came out.

I forced myself to calm down a little. I stopped, caught my breath, and wet my lips. I kept on whistling repeatedly, wandering in the general direction that I supposed my father to be. The late afternoon sun coming around the tree trunks made flashes of confusing light as I walked, desperately scanning the faces wandering around me, alone, whistling the family whistle.

Suddenly I heard—not just with my ears, but with every nerve in my body—my father whistling back. The heart in my chest exploded with joy.

I kept on whistling as loud as I could and kept walking. My father's whistle drew closer. There and then, in the woods just outside the village of Nisko, I saw—and I shall always see as long as I live—my father running toward me.

We hugged each other hard. Before this, I had never seen my father cry. For me, tears did not come. The well was dry. But he had pulled me back from a cold abyss that, until moments before, I never knew existed. I could still feel it at my back. But I was with my father again. And his rough laborer's coat looked better to me than the finest silk suit.

4

Escape

We wandered among the men who were now congregating loosely in groups of five or ten. They spoke in Yiddish. We passed near one group.

"I think we're not too far from the Russian zone. Maybe we should go east," a man said.

"How far is it?" another asked.

"I don't know. Thirty kilometers, maybe fifty."

We walked on and found another group where we recognized some men from Chorzow. We joined them, confirming with eye contact that each had survived. Gottlieb was there, the owner of the store where my mother bought shoes for Moniek and me. About fifty years old, he was six feet tall with an athletic frame and the narrow mustache popular at the time.

"I didn't see anybody dead or wounded," said Gottlieb.

"I didn't either," said my father.

"They must have been shooting in the air just to scare us."

"It worked," someone said. Other men from our city were now joining us.

One of them said, "Maybe we should work our way back to Chorzow."

"I don't think," interjected Gottlieb, "that the gestapo brought us here to allow us to go back with impunity to our families. The Germans will shoot us if we try to go back."

"He's right."

My father listened intently. "I suspect the first transport from our city probably went through the same thing we did," he said. "I don't know of anyone who returned. Does anyone know?" he asked the group. There was silence and shaking heads.

"No one returned," Gottlieb said, rubbing the stubble of his two-day beard. "I heard the Russian demarcation line is not too far away from here. I'm going in that direction. This war is not going to go on for long. I'd rather wait it out in the Russian side than go back or hide out here."

My father looked at me and nodded, meaning he agreed.

"I'm going with you," said one of the men, followed by two or three others. A few others wandered away toward another group. My father and I walked over to Gottlieb.

"We're going, too," my father said, putting his hand on my shoulder. He turned to me and said in German: "I have a feeling Salo and Josel did the same thing."

"Okay," someone joked, looking at our newly formed expedition to the Russian zone. "We now have a minion." (A minion is the minimum prayer group of ten men.)

I made a quick count and sure enough there were nine men in our group and me, a teenager, but a man according to Jewish custom.

We began walking east, avoiding the larger roads where we might encounter German soldiers. Many other groups walked in the same direction. Some groups then turned to the north, some to the south. No one walked back toward the field by the railroad tracks.

It was already dark when we approached a village. Gottlieb volunteered to go in to see if it was safe and if he could find a place where we could sleep. We waited in silence for about twenty minutes until he returned.

"I found a place we can sleep," he said. "There are no Germans here. I gave a pair of shoes to a farmer, and he will let us sleep in the stable. He was happy with the shoes. He even promised some milk and bread."

Only now did it occur to me that anything we had in our knapsacks was of great value, and I despaired that I had dropped mine when running away from the Germans. Fortunately, my father kept his. Though he lacked the currency of shoes to trade, he did have some clothes, a pack of needles, a spool of thread, and his tailor thimble.

We followed Gottlieb to the stable behind the first house in the village. On one side, there were some horses and farming tools. On the other side, there was a lot of hay and about a dozen bags of grain. There was enough room on top of the hay to accommodate all ten of us. As soon as I sat down, exhaustion nearly overcame me. I hadn't realized how tired I was. The sweet fragrance of the hay was welcoming.

The farmer came in with a half pail of milk and two loaves of bread. He handed it to Gottlieb, who thanked him in Polish. We shared the meal. As soon as I finished eating, I fell straight to sleep.

My father gently shook me awake about eight in the morning. Everybody else was already up. While I slept, my father had managed to barter his work shirt for a loaf of bread, a bottle of milk, and two hard-boiled eggs. We saved half this ration in the knapsack. With his pocketknife, he divided our breakfast portion and gave me the distinctly larger half. I was glad and eager to eat. Only three days before, I was home where food was plentiful and I never gave it a thought. Since then, I had been thinking about it constantly. Now, after my breakfast in the stable, I could easily have finished all we had in the knapsack. I understood—in my mind and in my belly—we could not be sure where we would get our next meal.

Gottlieb's voice broke my hungry reverie. "It's time to go."

Our group walked out together toward the morning sun, too worried about what lay ahead to reflect on what lay behind. Gottlieb had given us some leadership, but he could not know what lay ahead. He kept us on the dirt roads or walking through fields or woods most of the time. We did sometimes see German soldiers on the main roads. Whenever we approached a village, someone would volunteer to go in first to be sure the way was clear.

Late in the afternoon, we approached a village and learned that there were a few Jewish families there. Our group divided, each to try their luck individually. My father and I knocked on the door of a small cottage; two or three rooms. An elderly woman opened the door. She was stocky and small, like a typical Polish farm woman. Rather frightened, she looked at my father and at me, and said "What do you want?"

My father addressed her in Yiddish. "Excuse me, ma'am. This is my son. We are from Upper Silesia, and we are on our way to the Russian border," he said. "If possible, we would like to sleep here overnight. Any place under a roof. We'll be no bother to you." He paused. "Can you please help us?"

Her husband had appeared standing behind her. He had a large beard and was wearing a long coat and head covering that I saw many Jews wearing in Sosnowiec. In Yiddish, he said to his wife, "Ask them to come in."

We entered into the main room. To my surprise, it had a dirt floor. There was a wooden table and three chairs, a wooden cabinet, and a basin on another small table with a chair next to it. On the opposite wall there was a stove with a teakettle steaming gently. Kitchen utensils hung from the wall. An iron bed and a door leading to another room were close to the stove. The man and woman spoke to each other for a moment in hushed tones.

"You can sleep there," said the woman, pointing to the bed. "You can use the basin to wash your hands."

"Thank you," my father said.

"Would you like a glass of tea?" she asked.

"We don't want to bother you. It's very nice of you to let us sleep here."

"It's no bother. I have the tea ready." She placed three glasses and spoons and a cup filled with sugar on the table and poured the tea. Then she motioned us to the table. Her husband sat with us. We watched him stir sugar—less than a half-teaspoon—in his glass. My father also took a very small amount of sugar and fixed me with a purposeful stare to make sure I understood to do the same. I watched the sugar quickly dissolve in my glass then took a sip. It was hot; delicious. I felt the warmth spreading in my chest, the glow of the first hot food that I'd had in four days.

"Where are you from?" the man asked. My father told him. From the look on his face, it was obvious he did not know much about Upper Silesia or Chorzow. So, my father explained that we were about twenty-five kilometers from Sosnowiec.

"Oh, Sosnowiec! I know someone who came from there," he said.

My father told him about our city and that we owned a store and tailor shop.

"Then it seems you are not a poor man."

"Well," my father replied. "I was not a poor man." He told them what had happened to us and how we had decided to go to the Russian zone. "How far is it from here?" asked my father.

"Not too far. You can walk it in a day. This road will take you to the village of Rutki, which is on the border of the Russian zone." He explained the German patrols passed his village once a day, usually around ten in the morning. Even though thus far the Germans had not bothered them, he said it would be better if we left early in the morning. My father agreed.

That night, we slept in our clothes and used our coats as blankets. Next to my father, in the unexpected hospitality of the cottage, I was warm.

The man woke us around six in the morning. We washed in the basin with warm water from the kettle, and then went to the outhouse. It was a brisk, chilly morning. When we came back, the woman was moving about near the stove and we were surprised to find two glasses of hot milk on the table for us and two thick slices of bread with butter. I was hungry. Waiting for my father's lead, I gazed at this bounty—the steam rising from the milk, the delicious bread. He was hungry too, but never showed it. He turned to the man and explained that he had only a shirt or a pair of socks that he could offer for payment.

"No, no," said the man, waving both of his hands. "Keep your stuff. You need it more than we do."

So often, one says "thank you" as a simple courtesy. But then, when one is truly and deeply thankful, the words seem hollow and inadequate.

"Sit," the woman said, drying her hands on her apron. "Before it gets cold."

When we finished eating, we put on our coats and prepared to depart. We thanked them again and again. I pulled the knapsack up to my shoulder. Then the woman handed me a half loaf of bread and motioned me to put it in the knapsack, as if I was her own son. I was overcome. I stood mutely holding the bread, ready to cry. They were obviously poor and yet so giving to us, complete strangers. We thanked them profusely, unable to stop. The man just said "*gei gesunteheit* (go in good health)."

The defining moments in a lifetime do not always reveal themselves in the moment. But I know now that when I walked out of that cottage, I was a different person than when I walked in.

Before I walked in, if you asked me who I was, I would have said, "I am Polish." I went to Polish schools. Polish patriots and Polish heroes were my heroes. When Pilsudski, the first Polish president died, I cried for him. I was ten years old.

I would have said I was Jewish too, but second, not first. I had a basic Jewish education as a matter of form. But I admit that with my upbringing in Chorzow, I looked down on the religious Jews like those that I saw in Sosnowiec, like my cousins and, yes, like the man and woman who gave me food and shelter. I was not comfortable among them, feeling that in terms of education and sophistication, they were of a lower class. Our non-Jewish friends were quick to point out, when they talked badly about Jews, that they didn't mean Jews like us but rather those with long beards, funny head coverings and clothes. Those people were Jewish first and Polish second.

But it dawned on me, leaving the cottage on the road to Rutki, that the Poles had really never accepted me as Polish first. To them, I was a Jew like all the others. The gangs in the streets of Chorzow would always be on the prowl for Jewish boys to beat up. That had always been a daily reality for me, going to and from school. And now, a bearded man with a funny head covering had shown me human kindness in an hour of need. All because I was Jewish. The man and the woman—whose names I never knew, poor people in a poor village whose name I never knew—did more than the wisest rabbis of Chorzow. They showed me that I was Jewish first and Polish second, even though I had very little knowledge of what being Jewish was all about. If this seems like an insignificant change, it was not. To me, it was profound.

Sixty years later, I consider myself an American first. But that comes out of the uniqueness of this country of immigrants. The rest of the world is like a closed shop. Being a "real" German, you had to be an ethnic German. Being a "real" Pole, you and your father and his father had to be Polish natives. Everyone else was considered a stranger, a foreigner, a Jew, a gypsy. But in America, practically the whole country is foreigners and immigrants. Some are first generation, others second or third; so what? We're all newcomers, judged on merit and not parentage. Maybe you have to come from an "old country" to really appreciate how remarkable that simple distinction is: merit, not parentage. If my English has a Polish accent, still I don't feel any more foreign than anyone else here. I am an American, no less and no more than anyone else. Sure, there is anti-Semitism here, racism, crime, and many other ills, but it is perpetrated by individuals, not supported by law and legislation.

The man and woman who wished us "*gei gesunteheit*" so many years ago in the Polish countryside are long dead by now, even if they managed to escape the Holocaust. But the profound kindness they showed lives on in me, I hope, and in my children and theirs. Sometimes a half loaf of bread is brighter than the sun.

5

The Russian Zone

After we left the house of our hosts, we met Gottlieb, who had also learned about the village of Rutki on the border of the Russian zone. The rest of our minion gathered together, and we began walking east. I was still hungry, but the puzzling change in my life kept me from dwelling on the hunger too much. In my mind, to the rhythm of my walking, I tried to understand these perplexing feelings.

We arrived at Rutki around six in the evening. Gottlieb again volunteered to scout ahead while we all stayed low in the nearby woods. A half hour later, he returned with a smile. He found a farmer who would not only accommodate all of us, but who would also arrange for someone to take us across the border at night. There were no Germans in the village. They were all at the border station on the outskirts of the place. We were excited to be so close to our goal. Could it be that we would really escape the reach of the Germans?

After dark, we followed Gottlieb to a secluded farmhouse, bigger than the others we had seen in the village. As we arrived at the door, the farmer came out, a middle-aged, husky man. Behind him was a pretty, teenage girl with long, brown hair, who caught my attention instantly. We exchanged glances and subdued smiles. It was so refreshing for me to see someone my age—better yet, a girl. She wound up walking next to me as we followed her father to the barn behind the house. She said hello and greeted me with a smile so sincere that it brought a spontaneous smile to my face as well. She asked where I was from. But before we could converse much, our group settled down inside the barn.

Gottlieb and my father went off with the farmer to his house and, with a glance back at me, the girl went too. I found a place in the hay for my father and me to bed down. After a short time, the girl came back and, to my delight, invited me into the house. I told her my name, and she told me hers, Jadwiga.

We went in through the kitchen, where my father and Gottlieb sat at the table with the farmer and another man from the village. My father smiled when he saw me with Jadwiga. We went into a small, neat bedroom that she shared with her younger brother. I sat at a table that had some schoolbooks on it. Jadwiga asked if she could bring me a glass of tea or milk. Milk had never been my favorite, maybe because my mother constantly nagged me to drink it. But this time, without hesitation, I said, "Thank you. Milk would be fine."

She brought in two glasses and sat at the table with me. We chatted for quite some time. Well, I guess I was the one who did most of the talking. It was just so nice to speak with someone my own age and besides, she just kept asking me questions about my school, the city life, and what we did for fun after school. She knew from books that Upper Silesia was on the border with Germany and Katowice was the capital. But that was all.

I told her, with some pride, about the coal mines in the region and especially about the steelworks, the largest in Poland. She wanted to hear about the trolley cars, the train station, the paved streets. Her eyes went wide when I told her that cars had begun to replace the horse-drawn wagons. She had never seen a car. I told her that I never saw a cow in the city. The only time I saw them was when we went to the mountains on vacation. She was a good listener, sincere in her curiosity and always with that friendly smile. Now and then, she moved her head just so, to cascade her long, brown hair and shake it back over her shoulder. I would have stayed there indefinitely, except that my father poked his head in the room and said, "Siegfried, it's time to go. We have to get up early tomorrow morning."

"Thank you for the milk, Jadwiga," I said. "I really enjoyed our conversation."

I went out with my father. As I look back on it today, I realize, in our conversation, which must have been at least a half hour, not once did she ask if I was Jewish. She looked upon me as a boy from the city, not as a Jew. With her in my thoughts, I drifted to sleep.

After an interval of what seemed like fifteen minutes, my father roused me from my bed of hay. It was still pitch-dark.

"Get up," he said. He was holding a pail of water at angle, ready to pour some into my hands. "Here. Wash."

The cold water on my face woke me in a hurry. It was about three in the morning. Everyone else was awake. Some were drinking milk and eating bread. My father handed me a half bottle of milk and a big chunk of bread with some butter on it. While I slept, he had traded for some food. I had hardly finished eating when the man from the village I saw yesterday at the kitchen table walked in.

He waved his arm abruptly at Gottlieb and called out, "Let's go."

We all rose to follow him.

"Father, where's the knapsack?" I called, looking all around for it. He grabbed me by my arm.

"It paid for the food and the border crossing," he said.

As we filed out of the barn, it occurred to me that now we had absolutely nothing left to trade for food. The very thought made me hungrier. I looked up at my father. With tears in his eyes, he turned his head away from me. He understood what I was too young to really grasp. Here we were, about to cross the border into another country—destitute, penniless, and with absolutely no idea what was to become of us. Like the blade of a knife, he felt the torment of a good provider who finds he cannot provide.

It was so dark that we had to stay close to each other. Even though we couldn't see and didn't speak, I could feel the tension in our group. In less than a half hour, we reached a small brook, about ten meters wide, bubbling gently. We walked along the brook for a little while until we reached a place where the water was only about five meters wide and there were rocks protruding from it: our stepping-stones away from the Nazis. We stopped there and gathered close around the guide. He pointed across the brook.

"Here we are," he said quietly. "There is the Russian side. Go in that direction. You will see a road, which will lead you directly to Sieniawa. It's about five kilometers."

He nimbly crossed the brook, smoothly stepping from one stone to another. One by one we followed him across. There was a steep bank on the other side, about three or four meters high. He helped the first one of our group to climb by pushing him up. My father pushed me up first and when I got to the top, I bent down and grabbed his hand and helped him up. We helped some of the remaining members from our group. Our guide remained down in the streambed to help people up.

"Hey, he took my knapsack!" shouted the last man up. We turned around to see that the guide had already vanished. He had suggested that the man take off his knapsack to make it easier to climb. But instead of tossing it up, he stole it. And that was our farewell to German territory.

With Gottlieb in the lead, we walked through the darkness in the direction the thieving guide had indicated. His credibility had now suffered, but it was really all we had to go on. Soon we saw some lights in the distance, and we then came to a road. We followed it until we came to a fork where we stopped.

Gottlieb was tense. "He never said anything about a fork in the road," he declared.

The left side seemed to go toward the distant lights, which we assumed to be Sieniawa. Gathered close, our minion agreed to head for the lights. As we moved on, we saw some silhouettes of distant buildings ahead in the gloom. Then the road curved away from the buildings.

All at once, a loud yell—"*Postoi!*"—pierced the quiet, so abrupt it nearly made my heart stop. Two Russian soldiers approached with rifles leveled at us. I was happy they weren't Germans, but I was frightened just the same.

"*Kuda idiosh!*" they barked.

To my astonishment, my father stepped to the front and spoke to them. I didn't know until that moment that he really spoke Russian. Gottlieb also blinked in surprise.

Occasionally at home when my father was in a good mood, he used to sing Russian songs. Later on, I found out that some of those songs were Russian army songs and not the sort you sing to children. He learned Russian as a young man living in Piotrkow, Poland, when it was then occupied by the Czarist Russian army. He was even drafted into the army, a term that, at times, could be for many years of service. He was shipped to the city of Baku in the Caucasus, but fortunately in less than a year was able to go back home to Piotrkow.

My father told the soldiers we escaped from the Germans. They marched us to the nearby Soviet border station. They brought us into a large hall packed with refugees. There were at least fifty men, women, and children. Most had come from villages 100 or more kilometers inside German-occupied Poland. There was no one else from Silesia. As the night went on, more people were brought in, but the main hall was full and they were kept in the corridors. There was only one bathroom available for the refugees, and there was always a line of ten or twelve people.

In the morning, they set up a table in the corridor with a big samovar and loaves of bread in straw baskets. Three Russian soldiers stood behind the table. As we lined up for our ration, a Russian officer stood on a box to address us. Those few in the room like my father who understood Russian listened carefully while all the others stood in ignorance. When he finished, my father announced in a loud voice that they were going to let us go. He explained that the road led to Sieniawa, the nearest town. Then the soldiers at the table started to hand out cups of tea and what looked like a third of a loaf of bread, a very big piece. I was really hungry. The tea was scalding hot and there was no sugar, but I didn't mind. I finished off my portion of bread in no time, even though my father urged me to save some, as he did.

Then we went out again, our original minion still together, joining the stream of people walking. We could breathe a little easier because we no longer had to worry about German soldiers. A truck with Russian soldiers passed us on the road. They were singing aloud and they waved to us.

"What a difference," I thought, waving back.

Even though we did not know what awaited us, at least we knew the Germans wouldn't be there.

We walked for some hours before we reached Sieniawa, a small city. As we entered, I pulled out my handkerchief to wipe my face and noticed, squeezed in the folds of it, a two-groszen coin—a penny.

"Father," I said, holding it up. "Look."

He chuckled and took it from my hand. "How come you did not give it to the Germans?"

"I didn't know I had it."

We were now approaching the busy town marketplace. There were stands offering all kinds of things: food, clothing, tools, and sundries. We did not venture in since we had only the one penny and nothing to trade. One of the people from our group had learned that there was a public soup kitchen in the town. He gave my father instructions to get to the place. As we walked in that direction, we passed a stand with some food items and some candy on display. With a swift and agile stride, my father stepped up to the stand. Before I knew it, he turned around and handed me a single piece of candy he had bought with the penny. His face was beaming.

It was just an ordinary cherry-flavored candy, not even in a wrapping. But to me, it was purest ambrosia. I can never forget my father's face, his expression of love and satisfaction at seeing me enjoy the treat. In the bitter reality we faced, impoverished and hungry, we found a little drop of sweetness.

Abram Eichel

My father was born in 1881 in Piotrkow Trybunalski, Poland, not far from the city of Lodz. It was a small city, mostly Jewish. His parents, who owned a bakery, were not rich, but they were respected in the town. My father had three brothers and two sisters. The eldest was a girl, Gitel. Then came the boys, Yankel, Abraham (my father), Burech Hersh, and Froim. The youngest was his sister Rifka.

My grandfather died when my father was about ten. His mother Mindel stepped in to run the bakery in addition to running the household. She was known in the family as Mindel the Baker.

If my father was not the favorite child in the family, neither was he the bad apple. That distinction was shared by Burech Hersh and Froim (also called Benny and Philip). In 1905, they were arrested for anti-czarist activities and sent to Siberia. They eventually escaped and fled to America.

My father became a tailor. He married Chana Feiga Mayerowitz, and they got their own apartment in Piotrkow. Together, they worked long hours, but they barely made a living. In 1906, their firstborn, Lisa, came. Salo followed two years later. By then, it had become nearly impossible to support the family, so my father decided to move to Sosnowiec, Poland, which was on the border with German Upper Silesia. Upper Silesia was his real interest. He had been told that life there was "like God in heaven."

He worked as a tailor in Sosnowiec, and still had difficulty making ends meet. In 1914, early in the war, he was able to secure permission to cross the border to work in a coal mine in Königshütte. The army had begun to harvest the able bodied German men, and miners were needed to keep the war machine running. My father was anxious to take advantage of this opportunity for work, which was thought to be short-lived. Everyone said the war would be over by Christmas.

Life in Upper Silesia may have been like God in heaven, but my father began somewhat lower down. He took on the backbreaking work without complaint, digging coal out of a dark mine. Before long, he also organized a tailor shop catering to the miners and became the *meister* (manager). Working two jobs brought him a fairly good salary. He had an official pass that allowed him to travel back to Sosnowiec every weekend to see his family.

As I look back on it now, my father's coal mine experience shows something about him. I took it for granted all my life, but I now think it is a kind of miracle. This poor baker's boy who lost his father at a young age, why did he strive so hard? Why did he work twice as hard as others did? Why did he burn to seize his life and make more of it when most of the people around him were resigned to their lot? I don't know the answers. But I do know that this thing that drove his life became part of my life. It saved my life. Maybe a lot of boys think this about their father, but I think my father was heroic.

Josel was born in 1917. Shortly afterward, the family moved to Königshütte. The United States had entered the war that year. My father was among the many who felt this would swing the balance of power in favor of the Allies and lead to the end of the fighting. A year or so after it ended, my father quit the coal mine and opened up a custom tailor shop on the main street of the city. War-weary Europe just wanted to get back to work, and business was good. Eventually he converted the shop into a men's clothing store and moved the tailor shop to a less expensive location. But he was never the kind to revel in prosperity. He used to say, "God does not give with both hands. If he gives you something good with one hand, he will take something away with the other."

And, with one hand, God took away the health of my father's wife, Chana Feiga. Although he engaged the best doctors, she died in 1920. He was left alone with Josel, (age three), Salo (age twelve), and Lisa (age fourteen).

Two years later, he married my mother, Mania Russ, who had been living in Sosnowiec. She was thirteen years younger than her new husband was and came from a rather poor, but respected, family in Bendzin, a city near Sosnowiec. I don't know much about my mother except that she was a very attractive and smart girl. I also know, before she married my father, she had lived for a time in the big city of Warsaw. Jicryk, her brother, introduced her to my father. After some negotiation with her family, as was the custom in those times, the wedding plans were finalized. My father was considered to be rich, so my mother's family all felt she had married well.

From the beginning, my mother helped in the store. She quickly proved her business acumen, particularly in dealing with creditors, something he was not very comfortable with. She always told my father what to say to the creditors and also how to say it.

"Why don't you tell him yourself?" my father would reply. "You know how to tell me what to say. Why don't you take care of it?"

They argued frequently about this. But, as often as he objected, events always confirmed that she was right. Seldom did he acknowledge this, but my mother knew.

"He'll complain a lot," she said of her husband. "But he listens and does what I tell him to do."

I was born in 1924, my mother's firstborn. It was the height of my father's financial success, and I received an almost princely upbringing. I never felt that we lacked for anything. My father had season tickets to the opera. We lived in comfort and had a housekeeper by the name of Hannele. Of course, we were well-dressed. We usually spent our summer vacation in the mountains. We would rent a bungalow or apartment for July and August. My mother would take Josel, me, and, then later, my younger brother Moniek. Lisa and Salo would come over and stay for a week or two or perhaps over a weekend. Sometimes my father would come for a weekend as well.

Although my father was raised Orthodox, Judaism did not figure largely in our family. We observed the three main holidays—Rosh Hashanah, Yom Kippur, and the first day of Passover. I was reluctant to attend synagogue even on those few days. My religious education consisted almost solely of six months of private tutoring just before my bar mitzvah at the age of thirteen. In comparison to my religious cousins in Sosnowiec, I was considered illiterate and practically a *goy* (Gentile).

Between 1920 and 1930, my father managed to bring some of his relatives from Piotrkow to our city. At first, it was Gucia, the eldest daughter of his brother Yankel. Then he helped Yankel get a job in the coal mine and then bring his whole family. Yankel struggled financially. My father made the wedding for Gucia and gave her wedding dowry when she married Hassenberg. My father also helped bring over Sofie Chencinski, who was a sister of his first wife.

My mother gave birth to Moniek when I was four. It was a difficult labor. After that, my mother gained a lot of weight. As we grew, Moniek and I came to realize that my mother treated us differently than she did Lisa, Salo, and Josel. We were her babies. She sometimes bought us special treats like oranges, chocolate, or cake. She let us know it was just for us, not to share with the older ones. I was very unhappy about this. I felt my mother was not right. Lisa, Salo, and Josel always treated us no less than brothers.

6

Lvov

"Now!" my father said cheerfully after I enjoyed the cherry candy. "Let's see where we can get something to eat."

So, through the streets of a strange city I followed my father, a man who had already known much hardship in his life.

Before too long, we found the public kitchen of Sieniawa, which was brimming full of refugees. It was in a two-story brick building. The first floor was mostly one large room with a counter at the far end that opened into the kitchen. When we walked in, the room was full with maybe a hundred people there. Most were lined up against the wall, shuffling slowly toward the kitchen. Tables and benches were in the center of the room, and they were full.

When we got to the window, we were handed a bowl of hot soup and a chunk of bread. There were no spoons available so we had to sip from the bowl. There was no space at the tables, but we found standing room along the wall where we started sipping our soup and devouring the bread.

The group that had come with us to Sieniawa had dissolved, and we didn't see anyone we knew in the crowded room. My father learned from some of the other refugees that there was a room upstairs where we could sleep, so at least we'd have a roof over our heads for the night. It was only around seven in the evening when we finished eating, but we were exhausted. I think the daily uncertainty of life now sapped as much strength from us as all the walking did.

We climbed the stairs and found a large room with long rows of beds in the center, all occupied. I didn't care if I slept on the floor and I was ready to flop down on some open space near the door, but my father pulled me purposefully behind him to a place along the far wall. At the time, I didn't understand why the place he chose was any better than the one I chose, but it became evident pretty soon.

Within an hour, the room was full. Every inch on the floor was occupied. All night long, people were coming and going from the door and, in the process, stepping on the people near it. My father had positioned us where we were not disturbed. I admired his wisdom and slept soundly.

In the morning, he shook me gently awake.

"It is time to get something to eat," he said.

I climbed stiffly to my feet and stretched. The room was nearly empty. We went down the corridor to the bathroom to take our place in the line for the urinals and then in the line for the sinks to wash. There was no soap and we had to dry our face and hands with toilet paper.

Downstairs, we stood in line for oatmeal and bread. This time, we found room to sit at the table. Conversing in Yiddish with the people near us, my father learned that there were many Jewish families in Sieniawa, but they were hardly making a living themselves. He also learned that there were daily trains to Lvov, a large city. My father felt that since we were from a city, we would have a better chance to make a go of it in Lvov; to make a living and wait out the war, which he felt would not last long. He was told that the railroad station was on the outskirts of the town and that a lot of people travel without tickets by jumping on the train as soon as it started out from the station.

We thanked our neighbors and went directly to the railroad station. When we got there, we saw a throng of about fifty people waiting near the tracks just past the station platform. We joined them. A train arrived from Lvov with people on top of the roof and in between the cars. Some jumped off before it stopped.

The whistle on our train rang out. As it began moving out of the station, people ran along and jumped onto the steps of the cars. So did we. My father made sure I got on first, and then he hopped up behind me. Some people climbed up onto the roof. We stood on the steps until the train was moving at full speed. My father then opened the door, and we squeezed into the packed car. We had no choice but to stay next to the door because it was impossible to move forward. People were jammed in like sardines. We weren't worried about a conductor checking for tickets.

Fortunately, for all of us sardines, the train was an express to Lvov. The station there had been bombed, so the train stopped a few kilometers before it. We were glad when we could get out and draw a deep breath. We were in an area with many apartment buildings. We joined the crowd moving toward the city center. We were soon walking on a broad avenue. My father held my hand to be sure we weren't separated in the crowd of thousands that flowed like a river.

I didn't know what my father had planned as we trudged onward. I only hoped we could find the next soup kitchen because I was hungry again. Those past few days, we had moved with the crowd. We were almost like ants with the colony acting together, sometimes without any discernable leader making decisions. Many carried parcels and bundles; many were empty-handed, like us. At least we were happy to be away from the Germans.

The dull rhythm of the walking was broken all at once by a shrill note that came into my ear and exploded with recognition. It just couldn't be, but I swore I heard it. The family whistle! I would not have even dared to mention it to my father except, before the very first note ended, his hand pulsed abruptly against mine. He heard it, too! We froze in our tracks. The people walking behind us bumped into our backs. Simultaneously, we both answered the whistle and strained our ears like rabbits.

There! It came again! But how could it be? We walked forward, toward the sound, as we blasted out our reply. Again, we heard it, a little closer this time, and I recognized that it was Josel's whistle. Josel? Here? I jumped up again and again, straining to see over the heads of the crowd. We whistled to him, he whistled to us, drawing nearer.

In an instant, the miracle of sound became a miracle of sight as a figure burst through the crowd, seized my father in a hug, and lifted him up off the ground.

"Father! Father!" Josel cried as tears streamed down his face.

My father was struck dumb at the sight, speechless, almost uncomprehending. Josel then dropped my father, seized me like a bear, and nearly choked me against his chest. I cried and cried like a baby and locked my brother in my arms.

7

The Whistle

My father waited until I let go of my brother.

"Josel," he said, his voice rough from crying. "What about Salo?"

"Salo is fine!" Josel smiled. "In fact, when you first whistled back, I thought it might be him. But then I recognized it wasn't his whistle. Let's go to him now."

We began to walk with Josel. He had a distinctive, ambling gait, always a stroll in the park, never a care in the world. To see it again was a delight to me; it really was Josel. He really found us in the midst of that flowing mob of displaced humanity.

"What happened to you after you left home?" my father asked.

"Well, we reported to the Turnhalle in Chorzow," Josel began easily, like he was describing a casual afternoon picnic. The story he told was the duplicate of our own. Robbed by the Germans and chased away under the hail of machine gun bullets, they had crossed into the Russian sector at a town called Rawa Ruska. They had been in Lvov about two weeks. He was supposed to meet Salo in front of the Café de la Paix in the center of the city at one o'clock. Something had prompted him to take a stroll in the direction of the train station. That same something had further prompted him to try the family whistle over the heads of the incoming crowd, "just for the hell of it."

He made it sound like it was purely a whim, but, of course, it was more than that. It had not escaped his notice that the second wave of refugees into Lvov included both older men and younger boys and that perhaps my father and I were not safely at home where he had left us. Still, it was a miracle that he found us, against all odds.

"What time is it now?" my father asked.

Because we had all been liberated from the troubling necessity of wearing a wristwatch, we asked a passerby, who told us it was ten after one. Josel looked surprised. He said we still had a good fifteen minutes before we reached the city center, so we quickened our pace. I was worried. A minute ago, I had no thought of ever finding Salo. Now I was afraid of losing him.

"What if he isn't there?" I asked. "How will we find him?"

"Schmoy-boy," said Josel. "He'll be there."

From time to time, we passed bombed buildings. Except for the movies, this was the first time I had seen such a sight. Some of the interior walls were exposed. You could see how they had been painted or wallpapered. The clutter of bricks, plaster, and splintered wood lay in piles on the ground. One bomb from the sky and, in an instant, a home becomes a jagged graveyard. I wondered how many bodies were trapped in the rubble. While we were still back in Chorzow, I saw bombers in formation flying overhead every day, going deeper into Poland. We heard on the radio news that various Polish cities were bombed, especially Warsaw. But I never thought of the consequences. This was an ugly, gruesome picture. It sent a chill through me.

We turned on to a wide boulevard called Legionowa that had trolley tracks and wide sidewalks. Some men and women sat on the sidewalk with their backs resting against the building. Occasionally I saw someone spread out and actually sleeping on the sidewalk. I had never seen that in Chorzow. One might see a drunk or a beggar sitting on the street, but never sleeping there. And these people who we passed were not drunk or begging. They were just like us. Josel noted the population of Lvov before the war was around 300,000. Now it was home to an additional half-million refugees.

He had just opened his mouth to tell us we were approaching the café when Salo burst from the crowd, just as Josel had done. His face showed complete shock as he held father at arms length in disbelief. With another flood of tears, we exchanged hugs while Josel stood grinning. Suddenly Salo whirled on him.

"You were late!" he wailed, pushing Josel's shoulder. "You've never been late before. I was worried sick!"

Josel smiled and cocked his thumb toward us. "Their train was late."

Salo shook his head and turned to my father. "That's Josel."

This was only the latest outlandish thing in Josel's history. There were many others.

Josel Eichel

As a boy, Josel was generally troublesome; a poor student who often fought in school. He was rebellious and did not listen to my mother or Hannele. He spent most of his time after school with the kids on the street. It was a rough crowd, and no one was rougher than he was. My father may have wondered sometimes how Josel could be so different than the rest of us.

Of course, looking back on it from today, if we see a little boy who lost his mother when he was three and whose father always worked, we would clearly recognize that as a recipe for potential difficulty. But at that time, even though Dr. Freud was working in Vienna, the world was not so widely aware of these things as we are today. We didn't know why Josel behaved the way he did. It was a mystery.

It was about the worst when Josel was in *gymnasium* (high school). One day, a man who lived on our street came to the house.

"Herr Eichel," he said to my father. "My window has been broken. A ball came through it. I think it was your Josel. I would like you to pay for it."

"Did you see Josel do it?" my father asked.

"No."

"Then how do you know it was him?"

"Herr Eichel, who else on this street would break a window," he reasoned.

My father agreed and paid him. That was Josel's reputation.

Then later, there was the visit from the director of the *gymnasium* when Josel was in his second year there.

"Herr Eichel, I know you are not a poor man, but, no matter how rich you are, I cannot believe you would want to waste the money on keeping your son in the *gymnasium*."

He told how Josel was the only student who entered the schoolyard not through the door, but by climbing over the wall. Then, most often, he jumped down on the back of a professor. He never troubled about his studies at all.

My father removed him from school, no doubt to his great enthusiasm, and apprenticed him to a locksmith in our city. He applied himself to this trade in the same way he applied himself to everything else, that is, not at all. He disappeared for hours at a time to run with his friends in the street. This experiment in gainful employment came to a swift end, and his job was only to lay about the house. Of course, the trouble only escalated.

My father had a leather whip that he said was used by the Cossacks of Piotrkow. He used to joke that if we didn't behave, he would use it on us. Of course, he had never raised his hand to hit us. Josel got a hold of the whip. My brother Moniek and I watched him use a hammer and the iron railing of our balcony as an anvil. With an earnest industriousness I had not seen in him before, he painstakingly cut off the five lashes at the end of the whip. It was not easy because each lash had a wire on the inside. It was unthinkable to me to destroy something that belonged to my father. Moniek and I were fascinated. When he was done,

Josel carefully returned the whip to the place he got it. I never knew the consequences of that action.

Though my father never hit us, my mother did, sometimes with little provocation. She would slap us in the backside, not to hurt us, but to demonstrate disapproval. Not so with Hannele or Salo. When they slapped you on the backside, it hurt. However, the most frequent disciplinary action used by Hannele or Salo was banishment to stand in the corner, sometimes for a half hour or more. I very seldom got slapped or "cornered." But with Josel, it was almost a daily routine.

Now that I've said that my father never hit us, I must recall the exception to the rule.

Josel and his street friends loved to go to the *kino* (movie theater), but he had no money to pay for a ticket. Sometimes he'd pilfer empty bottles that we saved for redemption, and he'd collect the money himself. But this did not amount to more than maybe thirty or forty groszen, barely enough to go to a movie. Most often, he'd try to sneak in. Sometimes he'd make it and sometimes he wouldn't. Then my father had to go and pick him up.

My mother used to keep cash in a drawer in our linen cabinet. The drawer was always locked, and she was the only one who had the key. One day, she came screaming to my father that the money was missing. It was ten or twenty zlotys, which at that time was a lot of money. Suspicion quickly fell on Josel.

"Nein!" he replied emphatically. "No! I didn't even know there was money in there."

My parents did not want to believe he would steal. In our family, stealing was beneath our dignity. To steal from the family was all but unforgivable.

So, they believed Josel did not steal the money. Reluctantly, they questioned Hannele. We trusted her implicitly, but my father asked her bluntly if she took the money. She was stunned to be accused, invoking the heavens and Jesus Christ, she was ready to swear on the Bible. My parents believed her too and hastily apologized for ever doubting her. My father looked keenly at my mother.

"Are you sure the money is missing?" he asked.

"Of course, I'm sure of it!" she nearly yelled. "Do you think I would cause all this trouble if I wasn't sure?"

The crime was unsolved.

A day later, my father happened to pass the movie theater. He saw Josel and a crowd of friends exiting the theater. The minute they spotted my father, the friends scattered, disappearing in every direction through the streets. My father stood like a statue and glared at Josel. Josel's face turned red, and he slowly approached my father. They walked home, both in silent agony.

When they got home, I saw my father search Josel's pockets. He found a large number of zlotys in both coins and paper money. The mystery was solved. Josel had lied. My father's face turned dark with rage, and he slapped Josel hard across the face. Josel fell crying to the floor, covering his face. Then my father took off his belt and swatted him full force across the back.

"You're a liar!" He struck his son again. "You're a thief!"

The blows rained down hard, and Josel cowered and screamed. I was astonished. Luckily, my mother walked in at just that time.

"Abram!" she rushed forward and stayed my father's arm. "What are you doing?"

"He stole the money," my father moaned. He lowered his arm and turned to walk slowly out of the room, hanging his head. "My son is a thief," he whispered incredulously, shaking his head in pain and disbelief.

My mother helped Josel to his feet. He was crying pitiably. Hannele gently helped him take off his shirt, and they examined the red marks on his back. They led him away to his room. The silence echoed in the room, and I was in shock at what I had seen.

For the next few days, Josel sat at home most of the time and was very careful not to get in anybody's way. Every day there were discussions between my parents about what to do with Josel. Lisa and Salo sometimes joined in. Sending him back to school was rejected, as was attempting to apprentice him in another trade in our city. They agreed the influence of his street friends was the problem. It was decided it would be best to send him away from the city; to send him away from home.

And so it was that one day, upon returning from a business trip, my father announced he had found a place where Josel could live and learn a new profession. The place was a small town in the middle of Poland called Wloszczowa. It was near the city of Radomsk, where we had some relatives on my father's side. Josel had been apprenticed to a barber.

The barber was a poor, Jewish man whose family lived in a small apartment at the back of the barbershop. My father had made a written agreement, contracting for three years. Josel would work, sleep, and eat there while learning to be a barber. My father agreed to pay 300 zlotys annually. Josel would come home only for the High Holidays of Passover, Rosh Hashona, and Yom Kippur.

About a week later, my father took Josel to Wloszczowa. I will never forget that day. It seemed that everything happened in slow motion. Everyone in our house was sad and had tears in their eyes. So did I, even though I really couldn't grasp the full significance of what was happening. My father was deeply sad, too. He held open the door and Josel, holding his suitcase, walked out.

Holding the door, my father said quietly into the room, "There's nothing else I can do." He went out and gently closed the door.

He came back the next day, alone. There was a lot of soul searching going on for a while, especially at dinnertime.

"I wonder what Josel is eating today?"

"What happens if he gets sick?"

"Maybe we should have waited longer."

"What if he doesn't like barbering?"

But after a while, that talk diminished and we all got used to the idea that Josel was not with us.

A few months later, my father visited Wloszczowa as part of another business trip. We waited anxiously for his return. When he walked in the door, we didn't even let him get his coat off.

"How is he? How is Josel?"

"I didn't recognize him," my father said, smiling broadly. "It was a new Josel. He looked happy, and he loved everything I brought him."

He had brought cookies and chocolate. He said Josel was eating well and liked his job. The master told him Josel was very well-behaved and was learning well. It seemed to be a miracle. There was immense relief in our home. My father talked about Josel for days.

When Passover came, Josel came home and we could see for ourselves that my father was right. He was different; much more quiet and reserved.

At the Passover dinner table, he smiled and regaled us with tales of his dinners in Wloszczowa; how they served soup in large bowls and the potatoes were piled so high that it reached his nose without having to bend down. My mother gave him at least a double portion of *knedlech* (matzoh balls), and he still asked for more. His reformation was so dramatic that there was some talk about whether he should even go back to Wloszczowa. But my father decided it was best if he finished his apprenticeship, then came home.

After another visit there, my father told a story: he and Josel were riding through the town in a *droszka* (horse-drawn carriage) late one night. My father wanted to light a cigarette, but found he had no matches. Josel asked him for a few groszen, stopped the carriage, and walked over to the door of a store that obviously was closed. He knocked at the door and waited. My father was getting nervous; it was the middle of the night. Finally, the door opened and a few seconds later, Josel calmly returned to the carriage with a box of matches.

"What?" my mother laughed. "For a penny they opened the store in the middle of the night?"

"Yes," my father said. "And, for his father, Josel got the matches."

After completing his three years of apprenticeship, Josel came back to Chorzow. He was now almost eighteen years old. The new, subdued Josel was no longer interested in his old street friends. After a week or so, he started a new job at a local barbershop. He made a few new friends, and they were working people like him. Josel was no longer a problem in our family.

8

The Black Market

"All right," Josel said as we stood in the street after our reunion in Lvov. "Let's get something to eat. Come on."

We began to walk down the street.

"This place is too expensive," Salo explained, gesturing back toward the café where we met. I assumed they were taking us to a soup kitchen, but we walked a few blocks then entered another café.

"We have no money," my father whispered to Salo.

"Yes, we do," said Salo, leading us to a table.

I do not remember exactly what we ate. It was like a strange dream; so familiar yet so impossible. Dining in a café? With Salo and Josel? The whole day was a miracle. My father and I had awoken that morning on the floor of a soup kitchen. To find accommodations as good as that again was our highest aspiration. Now this: reading a menu; choosing a meal.

As we ate, Salo told their story. He and Josel had arrived in Lvov by train from Rawa Ruska about two weeks ago with Hassenberg and Hirsch, who were like part of our extended family.

Hassenberg was the husband of my cousin Gucia, Uncle Yankel's daughter. About forty when the war broke out, Hassenberg was a slightly overweight man of few words and a leisurely demeanor. He was a shoemaker and had a workshop on Ulica Swientego Jacka, just around the corner from where we lived. He, Gucia, and their two daughters, Regina (age eight), Mia (age five), lived in a room in the back of the workshop.

Hirsch was almost like an adopted brother. He came from a small *shtetl* (village) in Poland; a place where the standard of living was considerably lower than ours in Upper Silesia. He was drafted to the Polish army and was stationed in the barracks on the outskirts of Chorzow.

On High Holidays, the Jewish soldiers were allowed to attend synagogue. It was customary to invite a soldier to family dinner after the service. Hirsch was invited to our house every holiday while he was in the army. He was a slight, young man who had a warm way and was very good at telling stories. We all got to like him. When he finished his term, he asked my father if he could work in our tailor shop. Before joining the army, he had worked as an apprentice for a tailor and had learned how to make pants. At that time, my father's business was doing well. He was frequently giving out work to other tailors. After talking it over with my mother, Hirsch was hired. After my sister Lisa married and moved out of our house, Hirsch came to stay with us and slept in her bed.

Hirsch was the only one who did not give the Germans all of his money when they were robbed at Nisko. He still had some coins in his pocket when he arrived in Lvov with Salo, Josel, and Hassenberg.

Their first evening, just before it began to rain heavily, they wound up near the Cafeteria Warszawska. A bowl of cereal soup was fifteen groszen. Hirsch had enough for two bowls, which the four men shared. They remained until closing time, looking out at the dark rain, the only ones left in the place.

The manager came over to their table. Salo explained to him their predicament and asked if he knew of a place where they could stay overnight, out of the rain. The manager took a moment to look over the unshaven, shabbily dressed young men. He saw the unmistakable, worried look of refugees on their faces. He told them to wait a moment and went back into the kitchen.

When he returned, he told them they could stay overnight. He walked them out to the lobby, which was ringed with couches where they could sleep, and gave them a plate of sliced bread and a cup of butter.

"Stay here." he said. "And don't go into the cafeteria or kitchen."

He showed them where the bathroom was. The men thanked him so much he had to wave his hand to make them stop. He went out and locked the front door behind him.

He returned the next morning at six o'clock and found them awake and waiting in the lobby. The streets were still wet, but the four refugees were dry and thankful. Soon they detected the luxuriant smell of coffee brewing. The manager set them up at a table in the back and served them coffee and more bread and butter.

"When you are finished, you must leave," he told them. "You can try going to the churches or synagogues. They probably are already overcrowded, but you can try."

After the meal, he showed them to the back door and wished them good luck.

"He was an exceptionally nice guy," recalled Salo.

While Salo spoke, Josel and I had been busily eating the lion's share of our meal. He and I were always hungry. Salo paused in his tale and joked, "*Iss ein bißchen mehr* (Eat a little more)."

So, Salo, Josel, Hassenberg, and Hirsch left the cafeteria and decided to split up to see if they could find food and shelter. They agreed to meet in front of the cafeteria at six o'clock in the evening. But their luck was not so good and for a few days, they had to sleep on the street. One day, while walking with Josel on Ulica Legionowa, Salo spotted a man he knew from the *gymnasium* in Chorzow. The man recognized Salo too, and they shook hands.

The man was very well-dressed; not a refugee. He was also Jewish and the son of a well-known storeowner in Chorzow. He explained that, a few days before the war started, his father decided to take his family to a town not far from Lvov where they had relatives. They never had a chance to go back. He was in Lvov on some business and was leaving that afternoon. Looking at his watch, he apologized that he didn't have much time. Salo told him briefly of what had happened in Chorzow and of his current predicament. Not hesitating, the man pulled out twenty zlotys, a lot of money, for Salo. He suggested Salo and Josel go to the city market plaza where they may find some people from Chorzow doing business.

Wishing them good luck, their benefactor departed. Salo and Josel decided to split up and look for a place they could sleep, planning as usual to meet at six in the evening in front of the cafeteria.

At that hour, Salo was waiting with Hassenberg and Hirsch when Josel arrived. He had found an apartment house on Skarpowa Street where the superintendent was willing to let them stay in the empty coal storage room in the basement. The room was empty because coal was almost impossible to get at that time. The superintendent wanted ten zlotys per month, paid in advance. They decided to take it.

There was one small iron bed in the room and a small window facing the street. They found a wooden bench and some wooden boxes in the basement and placed them next to the bed. This made it possible for all of them to sleep with upper bodies on the bed and lower bodies on the bench and boxes.

The next day, Salo went to the city market plaza, as his benefactor had suggested. Sure enough, he bumped into a man he knew from Chorzow. He was peddling stockings and socks. He gave Salo a dozen pair in advance, told him how much he'd owe after selling them, and told him to work the far side of the plaza, so as to not infringe on his territory. Salo and Josel managed to sell all the goods that day and, after paying the man, they had a profit of more than twenty percent. They could pay for food. The next day, they picked up another dozen.

Now that we had caught up with Salo's story and Josel and I had stopped eating, we left the cafeteria. Salo took my father back to the apartment to rest. I went with Josel to the market. He still had a few pairs of stockings and socks to sell.

The market square was in the middle of the city. It was a big plaza with many stands displaying many different items, including food, clothing, tools, and every other type of gadget. The place was crowded with people walking between the rows of stands. Josel opened one pair of stockings and let them hang over his arm. As we walked he would shout from time to time, in Polish, "Ladies' stockings! Only two rubles!"

There were many other peddlers and their mingled voices made a bubbling cacophony. The price by the peddler was always slightly lower than the same item at the stand. Josel explained this was not legal, so we had to be careful to not be seen by a patrolling policeman and avoid getting too close to the stand with the same items. So, whenever we were getting close to such a stand, Josel just covered his hand with his coat and would not shout.

Literally, hundreds of other people like us were roaming the market with the same things we were trying to sell. However, in the weeks that followed, we consistently managed to sell all we had and sometimes even had to go for another pickup. We also found a baking factory where we could buy boxes of cookies at relatively low prices and could sell them much easier, but we had to pay up front. We would buy only three or four boxes at a time. On a good day, we made four trips to the bakery.

It was not easy to sell. People stopped to look at the stockings and tried to bargain. By the time it grew dark on my first day at the market, Josel managed to sell two pairs, making one ruble as profit. We left the market and went to the apartment.

Our basement room was gloomy, with one little dirty window facing the street where you could occasionally see the legs of people passing by. The floor was filthy with coal dust. Hassenberg had managed to find another place to sleep, so it was the five of us (Salo, Josel, Hirsch, Father, and me) that shared the bed. Considering the places we had slept since leaving home, this was pretty good. The best part was the cold-water sink. we could at least wash and have a drink. Some rags that did not look that clean and handkerchiefs had to substitute for towels.

The next day, Salo said that he was going to start looking for a job. Any kind would do, but it would preferably be in tailoring. I would now work with Josel in the market, and my father would help as a lookout. I was very glad to be included in this plan. After all, I could work like a man and help us get along. But there was a part of the plan I did not like at all.

My father told me to give Salo my long overcoat and I would wear his short laborer's coat. To answer my mute, incredulous expression, he explained Salo needed to be more presentable if he was to find a job. No matter how my father justified this, I felt terribly hurt. After all, he hadn't made me wear this coat when the Germans forced us to leave Chorzow, so why now? Our circumstances may have drastically changed, but I guess my likes and dislikes did not necessarily follow. I didn't think for a moment about the obvious practicality of the suggestion. I only sulked. I was convinced that, just like Lisa used to be my father's favorite child (we all knew it), he now liked Salo more than me.

A few days later, someone gave Salo the name and address of a tailor named Heller who was looking for help. He lived with his wife and small child in an apartment house and used one of the rooms as a workplace. Salo must have made a good impression because he got the job and started the next day. He was the only employee, and Mr. Heller and his wife took a liking to him. They even set up a bed in the workroom where Salo could sleep.

The fact that Salo now had a good-paying job gave a boost to our morale and also to our standard of living. Now that we had a steady family income, we could afford the luxury of going to the bathhouse once a week for a shower and steam bath. We had not bathed properly since we left Chorzow. We probably smelled and did not even realize it. As a kid, I never liked bathing or showering too much but this time a hot shower felt heavenly. I remember the steam room had wooden steps. The higher you climbed, the hotter the steam. My father slowly climbed up the six steps to the top and stayed there for a while. Josel and I could barely stay on the second step.

Though Hassenberg did not share our room, we stayed in touch with him regularly. He had found a job in construction and was renting a room in a family apartment. A few weeks after we arrived, Hassenberg told us about another tailor job. The owner of Hassenberg's apartment was a police officer who worked at a former Polish army building that was now occupied by the Soviet Police. He told Hassenberg they were looking for tailors who could fix the piles of civilian clothing left behind by the Polish army recruits. They were shipping some of the clothes back to Russia and also sold some on the black market. That was how my father found a job. Now we started looking for a room or even a small apartment to rent. However, it was not easy in a city overrun with refugees where half the buildings had been bombed.

The Soviets were offering good jobs in factories somewhere in Russia, but you first had to register and accept Soviet citizenship. Many homeless refugees were registering. Within a day or two, they were provided with transportation back to Russia. Though we were tempted by this, we refused to take Soviet citizenship. That would mean we could not go home to our family in Chorzow after the war, which, my father still believed, would not be very long.

Hirsch did not agree. He registered and was given a job in Dniepropietrkovsk, Russia. Before he left, we had a farewell dinner together at the Cafeteria Warszawska. Salo had tried to persuade Hirsch to stay, but he went, with thousands of other refugees, for the promise of a better life. Hirsch believed the life he had envisioned for himself would never be possible again.

Salo too knew what it was like to have plans and hopes dashed to pieces. It had happened enough to him in his life.

Salo Eichel

He was born Alexander Eichel on May 18, 1908, in Piotrkow Trybunalski, Poland, near the city of Lodz. When the family moved to Königshütte, Germany, he went to the Jewish *volkschule* (public school) for several years. Then he was accepted to the Staatliche Oberrealschule (high school). The family became thoroughly integrated into German life, and Salo liked it. They were secular Jews and so did not stand out as being different from the non-Jewish Germans, some of whom became family friends. My father Abram was now called Adolf, and his eldest son, Alexander, was called Salo.

Salo was an excellent student and was also on the school athletic club, being particularly skilled in gymnastics. He also had a good singing voice and belonged to the choir in the synagogue.

Just as he was attending the last year in the Staatliche Oberrealschule, the newly vested Polish authorities were gradually converting or closing German-speaking schools and urging the students to switch to the Polish schools. They spoke to my father and "asked" him to transfer his son to a Polish-speaking school. My father deliberated and decided it was not worth swimming against the tide on this issue, so he agreed. Salo was heartbroken and tried to resist but ultimately he had no choice. He switched to the Polish school. However he was so embarrassed in front of his German friends and his pride was so hurt that he dropped out of school altogether just before graduation. My father could not persuade him to complete his studies.

Salo was initially apprenticed to my father's friend Spitzer who had a wholesale piece goods business in our city. But Salo did not like doing menial work in the shipping department. He persuaded my father that he should learn tailoring to continue the family business. My father agreed, and wanted him to learn in a well-known, high-quality shop. He knew the person who owned just such a tailor shop in the city of Beuthen just across the border in Germany. He arranged for an apprenticeship for Salo. At that time, people living in Upper Silesia could easily receive passes and travel across the border without any problems. That is how Salo became a professional, custom tailor.

After his apprenticeship, he got a job as a tailor at the firm Salomon Salmonowitz in the city of Hindenburg, Upper Silesia, Germany, which was less than an hour by train from Chorzow. Salmonowitz was a German Jew, who, in addition to a tailor shop, also had a wholesale distributorship of men's clothing. Salo worked and lived there, earning a nice salary. He used to come home for weekends and holidays.

Salo always dressed well and was known as a charming cavalier. As a young man, his social activities often kept him out late and this, as I've said, resulted in the creation of the family whistle, so that he could get back into the apartment late at night.

I remember hearing my father criticizing Salo for spending too much money on his clothing, especially once when he bought a very expensive necktie. I don't remember what the exact cost was, but it must have been way above what my father thought he should pay. There was so much argument about this that I could not resist; I crept into Salo's room, looked into the drawer, and saw the tie. Sure enough, it somehow looked better than all the ties I had ever seen. It was rich, brown silk with vivid, gold stripes.

Most of Salo's friends, like Lisa's, were rich or from well-known families. I remember, after Lisa got married, there was talk about it being Salo's turn. He was dating Bela, one of the most glamorous and richest Jewish girls in town. But his hopes were destroyed again when her family suddenly moved to Spain. Salo was heartbroken. He was considered quite a catch and many attempts were made to interest him in other girls, but they all failed.

In 1938, his boss Salmonowitz advised Salo that he was ordered by the German authorities to fire all Jews. Because Salo was not a German citizen, he had to return to Poland. He moved back in to our house and worked with my father.

9

Brigidka Prison

A few days after Hirsch left Lvov, the superintendent of our building told us we could no longer stay in the room. The police were inspecting the buildings in the neighborhood, and it was illegal to rent a coal storage room for occupancy. He gave us one day to move out. That was a real crisis. It was Hassenberg again who came to our aid, giving us an address of a one-room apartment that we were able to rent immediately. The problem was that the apartment would not be available until the following day. That meant we had no place to sleep that night.

My father was allowed to sleep with Salo for the night. Josel and I had to find a place on our own. We found nothing and ended up falling asleep on a trolley car. In the middle of the night, at the end of the line, the conductor woke us up and said we must get off. It was raining heavily. I was sore from the trolley bench, exhausted and disoriented. I began crying. But Josel was charming when he explained our predicament to the conductor and he allowed us to stay.

When he left, Josel tried to cheer me up by saying, "Look at the bright side of this deal, kid! We don't have to sleep on the street and get wet. Tomorrow, we have our own apartment."

He made me feel better. I stretched out on the hard, wooden bench and went back to sleep.

The next day, we moved in to the one-room apartment. It had two beds. I slept with Josel, and my father had the other one. Salo continued to sleep at Heller's place.

Josel had started to look for a job in a barbershop. It was not easy for a refugee to find a job. The local people viewed refugees as thieving, dirty, and a threat to their health and safety. I must admit, when you are homeless, hungry, cold, and shivering, you do not consider stealing to be a crime. Just the opposite: it may be the only option you have to survive.

A few days later, Josel found a job at a barbershop. Things were looking brighter. Salo, Josel, and my father all had an income, and we had secure lodgings. I was fifteen and a half. Too young to work, by my father's judgment. And now that Josel had a job, my father did not want me to work the black market alone, even though I was doing pretty well selling cookies. It was getting more dangerous. The police were raiding the market plaza more frequently and locking up those without identification. But I was frustrated; I wanted to work too. I knew I could pull my weight like the others did.

Soon we were all able to dress better. We managed to buy new underwear, and my father fixed for us some clothing from the place where he worked. We no longer looked like homeless refugees. Only then did I realize that to be treated with respect, you had to look, dress, and behave respectfully. I realized my father was right when he told me to give Salo my long coat. That surely helped Salo get the job.

I did the house chores in the apartment, and sometimes went along with my father to the barracks where he worked and just hung around there. One day, Salo took me along to deliver a suit and coat he made for a Russian officer. I received a tip of one ruble. That was the first time I earned money for real work. (We did not consider trading on the black market as worthy. It was something we all understood. Not so much that it was illegal, but it was demeaning and only a temporary necessity for survival.)

Hassenberg worked as a helper in a bombed building that was being restored.

One day, not long after Josel was hired, Hassenberg told my father, "The foreman on my job is looking for some additional help. I think Siegfried can get a job there. If it's okay with you, I will introduce him to the foreman."

I overheard this and didn't give my father a chance to reply. "Father, I want to go with Hassenberg."

He looked at me with a serious, sad expression for a long moment, then turned to Hasssenberg. "Okay. Make sure you look after him. And I don't want him to do heavy work."

"Don't worry," he replied. "All we are doing is sweeping the floors and taking out the trash."

The next morning, I dressed early and felt excited to be going off to a real job. Hassenberg picked me up, and we went off to a brick, three-story apartment building that had been damaged by fire. The first floor had a few stores, which had already been renovated. We went up to the second floor, and Hassenberg introduced me to the foreman. He told me to wait, and he sent Hassenberg off into another room. The foreman asked my name and address, told me what my pay would be, then walked me over to the adjoining building and turned me over to the foreman there.

There were about twenty people working there in different rooms. Some were fixing the walls; others were fixing the windows. In some rooms, they were painting. The foreman took me to one of the rooms, which looked freshly painted and told me to pick up all the trash left on the floor and carry it down to the big container in front of the adjoining building. I eagerly began working.

It was only my second or third trip out to the trash container when I noticed a half-dozen police officers with rifles marching toward the building. I hurried back upstairs. The foreman was talking to a uniformed Russian officer. A few minutes later, the police officers with rifles arrived and the officer announced that all people on this floor were under arrest! We were to stop what we were doing and slowly, one at a time, walk down the stairs. I was stunned. The foreman motioned to us to go. On the street, we lined up in rows of three, accompanied on all sides by the police officers with rifles. I looked around for Hassenberg, but he was not here. About eighteen people were arrested, including the foreman. As we walked, it was obvious that nobody knew why we were arrested. People on the street occasionally shouted "What did you do?" or "Where are you going?" We only shrugged our shoulders or murmured, "Don't know."

We were marched toward the infamous prison called Brigidka, a couple miles from where we were arrested. I could clearly see the prison building a few hundred meters down the road.

I suddenly heard someone yelling, "Siegfried! Siegfried!"

I saw Salo, panic stricken, trying to get closer, but the police officer pushed him back. Until that moment, I think I was more puzzled than worried. But after I saw Salo—he seemed to be crying—I became very worried. I waved to him and tried to appear nonchalant. As we entered the prison, I was suddenly terrified, wondering if I would ever get out again.

We were lined up against the wall in a long corridor and one by one ushered into a room. There was a middle aged man in civilian clothes, sitting behind a desk.

As I approached the desk, he asked me in Polish, "What is your name?"

"Simon Eichel."

"Give me your passport."

"I don't have one, sir. I am a refugee." He asked for my address, then asked to see my hands.

"These are not the hands of a worker. What were you doing there?"

"Today was my first day. I was told to take out the trash."

"You weren't working yesterday?"

"No, sir. I was home." He then asked my age, took my fingerprints, and told me to leave through another door. It led into a much larger room with benches. There, I saw some of the other workers who were being arrested, sitting on the benches. A few police officers stood guard. No one spoke.

From time to time, another person from our group would walk in. We sat there for three hours. Then they led all of us into the yard and made us line up in single file. A police officer came in with a German shepherd dog on a leash. He put a rag up to the nose of the dog and then brought the dog over to our line. The dog was agitated, moving it's head back and forth and straining against the leash. He sniffed the first person in the line and then the next. I was near the middle of the line. When the dog came to me, I was afraid. First, he sniffed my shoes, then he excitedly poked his nose at my pockets. I thought he was going to bite me, but I was relieved when he moved on to the next person.

A few people after me, the dog began to bark ferociously and had to be restrained by the policeman. That person was hauled out of the line and taken away. After the dog finished, we were led back to the same, silent waiting room. Then, after about an hour, we were told we were free to go. My heart leaped up, and I forced my feet not to run out of the prison.

Outside, my father, Salo, Josel, and Hassenberg were waiting for me. When I saw the tremendous relief on their faces at seeing me, I almost cried. Hassenberg never looked so relieved in his life. While everyone hugged me, he explained, the previous night, there was a break-in and robbery of the clothing store in the building where I worked. The police suspected it could be someone working in that building, so they simply arrested everybody.

So, at the conclusion of my first day of real work, everyone was convinced I had better stay at home. I didn't argue.

10

Siberia

By the summer of 1940, France had fallen and the Battle of Britain had begun. In Lvov, soon after my release from Brigidka prison, the Russians began rounding up anyone who did not have a passport and sending them to temporary work camps in Russia. There were many in Lvov like us who did not want to take Soviet citizenship, so the Russians were determined to solve the refugee problem their own way.

The police went knocking at the door of every apartment. They went house-by-house, day and night. Those who did not have a passport would be brought to the local police station. To make sure we did not get separated, Salo began to sleep in our apartment. We were not overly concerned about getting shipped to Russia. By that time, we had already heard stories of people who went there and wrote back that they were working and doing fine. We had not yet heard from Hirsch, but he had left only a month or two ago. We felt, as long as we didn't have to take the citizenship, we could return when the time was right. We still believed the war would end soon and we would be able to go back to Chorzow.

Sure enough, before long we were visited by the police late one night. They waited patiently as we gathered up all our belongings, which was not very much, and took us along to the station. They were not rough or abusive, just doing their jobs. We got there and joined a large crowd who was already squatted on floors, seated on benches, and lounging in different rooms. It was almost like a bus station where people went voluntarily; nothing like the experience of being rounded up by the Germans in Chorzow.

Hassenberg, who did not live with us, found out that we were all taken. He gathered up his belongings and ran to the police station to verify we were there. Josel and I were standing near the door when he arrived, and he saw us. He spoke to the police officer guarding the door.

"I am a refugee," he said. "No passport. I would like to go with this group. I have relatives here."

"Where do you live?" the weary police officer asked.

Hassenberg told him.

"That's in a different precinct," the police officer said. "Go to the police station there. They'll take good care of you."

"But they will send me somewhere else! I want to be with my relatives."

"It's not my precinct."

"I understand," Hassenberg said. "Thank you for your help." He took the police officer's hand and pressed a pack of cigarettes into it. "If I could be with my relatives in this group…"

The police officer nodded his assent, and he made out the paperwork to register Hassenberg. After that, we always ribbed him that he was the only refugee who had to pay to get arrested. We were all fairly lighthearted. We'd work for a while; so what? We wouldn't starve or be shot. Then we would go back home. But we had no idea of the true nature of the Soviet solution to the refugee problem.

Eventually, we boarded trucks that took us to a train yard on the outskirts of the city. I thought we would board normal train cars. I was surprised when they brought us to freight cars. But the Russians put many fewer people in a car than the Germans did and there were at least some crude attempts to hang a curtain hiding the bucket that would serve as our toilet.

I am not sure how long we traveled on that train, but we lumbered along for what must have been at least a week. We stopped two or three times a day, and we were allowed to disembark for food they distributed to us. At some stops, they let us run under the big water pump used to fill the locomotives. Josel and I stripped down to our shorts and ran around under the refreshing shower. The soldiers guarding us only made sure we didn't stray too far away.

On some stops, Russian men and women approached the train selling various fruits, milk, and even ice cream. They carried the ice cream in a bucket and dispensed a scoop or two onto a piece of paper. We joked about this rustic method, but the ice cream was inexpensive and it sure tasted great.

On and on the train went, traveling east. When we passed the city of Svierdlovsk, we realized we were pretty far inside Russia, near the Ural Mountains. Still, I was not concerned. I was only sixteen years old, the only kid my age on the train. I thought about my early school days in Chorzow.

Mala Ringelheim

I have a clear memory of my first day of public school. My mother accompanied me, and I carried a large cardboard cone filled with goodies, including candy, chocolate, and cookies. A lot of other kids also carried cones, but I remember that mine was the largest. I was only five years old, and I don't know why my parents chose to send me to school one year earlier than required. I guess I must have been a big boy.

There were basically three groups of students in the classroom. In the first group were those students that were smart and studied hard. To them, the most important thing was to get good marks on the report card. To that group also belonged the students that had well-known and rich parents, even though they were not all outstanding students.

The second and largest group considered school just another place to play and have fun. Studying was considered a necessary evil. I was in this group.

The third group, about four or five boys, did not concern themselves with academic performance at all and didn't care if they were left back. They frequently skipped classes. The only energy they expended was on devising excuses to explain to the teacher why they failed to do their homework assignment. Our teachers used for such occasions a thin whip. I remember from personal experience it was quite painful when you received a few smacks on your left hand. Sometimes you could not forget the beating for a few days.

Although students naturally gravitated into one of these three groups, we were basically all the same; all Jewish, all normal kids. But it was a fact that, during school hours as well as after school, you would hang around only with kids from your group.

I was not too good of a student; I just didn't care. The only reason that I did not have to repeat a class was more due to luck than knowledge, I think. My teachers used to tell my mother that I had a good head but I did not apply myself.

Because our school was rather small, we shared the classrooms with the girls. In larger schools at that time, boys and girls had separate classes. In our school, we had three rows of benches: two for boys and one for girls. On the girl's bench sat the best, and the prettiest student in the class, Mala Ringelheim. Even today, her name has a resonance for me. She was slender, with brown eyes and curly brown hair. During class recess, she was always surrounded by the boys and I never got close.

She came to our school when we were in fourth grade. Her family, like so many others at that time, came to Upper Silesia from mid-Poland. Even though her family was not considered rich, Mala acted very proud and snobbish. Her tactic for ending arguments was a dismissive "I know better than you." She acquired the informal distinction as the best student in the class within a few days after her arrival.

She lived across the street from us. She frequently visited her father's wholesale chocolate store that was across from our backyard, so I saw her all the time. But we did not speak to each other. I was not in her group, and I didn't dare approach her. She acted as if I did not exist.

I had a cousin, Richard Chenczinski, who was in class with me. (His mother was the sister of my father's first wife.) He and his mother frequently visited our house. He was one of the very best students in our class; firmly positioned in the first group. He was the only one from that group I dared to talk to, even that was mostly after school. During school, classmates always surrounded him. Even though he was always very friendly with me, I felt like an unwanted follower because his friends paid little attention to me. It happened more than once that, in my presence, they made a date to meet without asking me to join them. That was painfully embarrassing to me.

I was embarrassed, more bitterly, one day after school. Richard was visiting, and we were in my backyard when Mala passed us on the way to her father's store. She walked with a slow and proud step, her shoulders back and her head held high. Without hesitation, Richard approached her and began a casual, friendly conversation. With great apprehension, I eventually eased into the conversation, a banal chat about school and teachers. I could see she plainly liked Richard and enjoyed talking to him. But she completely ignored my words and never even looked at me. It was as if I was a phantom in my own backyard.

I was only ten or eleven years old, too young to understand real love, but it seems obvious to me now that I was in love with Mala Ringelheim. I used to sit at our living room window for hours, waiting for her to pass by. When she finally arrived, I felt my heartbeat accelerate. People always want the thing that is hardest to get, and that was the case with me too. I guess the fact that she was above my social class in the school presented an invisible barrier between us that made her that much more appealing to me.

Sitting at the window, waiting for Mala, I devised a way to speak to her. I prepared a script in my mind designed to break the silence between us. Then I positioned myself in the backyard at a time when I expected her to pass. When she came, I approached her, trying to seem casual but probably overeager. I tried to make my voice sound relaxed, but it came out tense.

"Hello Mala. Uh, do we have history class tomorrow?"

"Yes," she stated, without breaking her stride, without looking at me. And on she walked…so much for my careful plan of action.

My after-school neighborhood friends were all Gentile since we were the only Jewish family in our building. Our building was probably the nicest one in the neighborhood. People who lived in our building were generally considered to be of a better background and economic level than most of those in the other buildings on the same street. Many parents in our building, including my parents, did not want their children playing with the *buksen* (street boys). Hannele was under instructions from my mother to not let me play with these boys. So, the social groups with their invisible barriers not only existed in my school, but they were in the neighborhood and in society as well.

I suppose it's natural that parents want their children in the best company. Maybe they were right because the children from the poor families did not have as good of an upbringing as those from the richer families. Whether this was right or wrong, I did not know at the time, and it did not bother me. However, I must admit that my mother's continuous, daily pounding into my head not to go or play with some of the kids because they were not up to our level (*meinesgleichen* in German) resulted in my feeling higher than those boys.

Our next-door neighbor in the building had a son, Horst, who was a few years older than I was. We were very friendly with each other, and we used to play together frequently. Our parent's relationship was cordial, but less social. They hardly ever spoke to each other except the customary greetings when they met in the hallway or on the street. Horst and I used to spend many hours in his apartment or ours. We would occasionally argue and stay mad at each other for a while, but we always became friends again.

Every Christmas, I was invited to their apartment for dinner. Even though I would not get any gifts, I was just as excited as Horst was. They had a Christmas tree with many gift boxes under it. One year, when I was ten, Horst received an electric train set with a lot of accessories. I helped him and his father set up the rails, switching equipment, and train station. The trains ran around the entire room and under the Christmas tree. I remember how envious I was of Horst being Christian and getting such terrific gifts every Christmas. Our holidays were dull in comparison. All I ever got for Chanukah was five groszen (a nickel) each day we lit the candles. That just gave me just enough to go to a movie at the end of the eight-day holiday. A train set? I could dream about it, but I knew I would never get it.

I remember frequently bemoaning to myself, "Why couldn't we be Catholics? Then I would get expensive toys, too. And I would not have to worry about getting beaten up on the way to school by gangs of boys just because I was Jewish."

It happened often enough. When I was born in 1924, there probably were no more than a few hundred German Jews in Chorzow. By the time I started public school in 1929, there were more than 1,000 Jews and most of the new arrivals were from Poland. We already had a separate Jewish public school up to sixth grade. The Gentile public schools had eight grades. It was mandatory for all children to finish eight years of public school or finish six years and continue to *gymnasium* (high school). There were only six grades in the Jewish public school because most of the Jewish students would continue on to *gymnasium*. Those who didn't would transfer to the city public school for the seventh and eighth grades.

Occasionally, we ventured onto the street and joined other kids in playing soccer or a kind of stickball called *pallant*. Some of the kids on the street were much rougher and frequently engaged in fistfights. This group used foul language and sometimes spoke badly about Jews. I am not sure if they only did it in my presence just to tease me or provoke a fight.

I would usually avoid fights but a couple of times, when they addressed me personally as a "dirty Jew" or something like that, I would respond back with an insult. Occasionally, I would get into a fistfight, and I did not always win. A bloody nose—his or mine—would usually end the fight. Sometimes the other kids would encourage each of us to fight; sometimes they would intervene to stop it.

I was pretty good at playing soccer and pallant and that earned me some respect on the street. They knew I was not a sissy, but I was a Jew and they frequently made sure to point it out to me in the most insulting way. The word *Zyd* (Jew) was used as a sneer.

On my street, I felt fairly safe. On other streets, not so. There were two ways to go to school from my house. The shorter way was via Ulica Ligota Gornicza, but there you could pass some rough kids who would harass you yelling, "*Zyd, Zyd.*" They would sometimes attack, and you would really have to run to avoid getting beaten up. The longer way was via the main street, Ulica Wolnosci, but it also was the safer way. On the way to school, I would sometimes meet some other Jewish kids and then we would use the shorter way because we knew they would not dare start a fight if there were three or four of us.

When I was about ten, I was persuaded by school friends to join a Jewish juvenile Zionist organization called Betar. Up to that time, I knew very little—if anything—about the Zionist organizations. When I joined Betar, it was already very popular in our city. There were other Zionist organizations, but Betar was the largest. At that time, it was at its highest point of growth. They had a small building with a rather large yard and we met there on weekends. In my group, there were some of the friends from my school. My group consisted of about twelve boys around the same age and an adult leader. During our meetings, we would sing Jewish songs, hear stories about Jewish Zionist leaders and about Palestine.

Here I realized there is more to Jewish life than religion and the Torah. I began spending less time with my friends on the street and more time in Betar.

I was also getting friendlier with Richard. Our parents used to visit each other. I vividly remember his father playing cards with my parents on the balcony of our apartment during the summer and Richard and I sitting nearby, listening to some of the conversation and jokes. His father was a sick man, but he was a very jolly person. I believe he had cancer and died when I was about ten. The day of his funeral I had to stay home all day. My parents felt Moniek and I were too young to go to a cemetery.

After Richard's father died, we visited the Chencinskis more frequently and they came to our house more often than before. Richard and I became better friends. It was his friendship that gave me the incentive to study harder. Another incentive was Mala Ringelheim. If I could break into her group, then she would talk to me. There was a bit of a competitive atmosphere between Richard and Mala, each with their followers. They would occasionally engage in debate about who knew more. I knew that only our teacher's praise for good homework and good answers would earn me some respect from Mala, Richard, and their friends.

But then a newcomer arrived in our class. Ida Brecher came from Lvov, the daughter of a poor family. She was seated in one of the last benches in the girls' row right next to where I sat. From the start, Ida proved to be a significant competitor for the best girl student of the class. Soon it became difficult to tell who was better, Mala or Ida. This was not to Mala's liking. Even though she tried not showing it, one could easily notice that she didn't like this pretender to her throne. While Mala continued behaving in her usual proud manner, Ida was just the opposite. She frequently helped other students, and she even whispered answers when the teacher questioned someone nearby. Being new to the class, she was not yet familiar with the group divisions and so she felt no barriers. She was friendly and would engage in conversation with anyone who approached her. A group of girls and boys gathered around her that was much larger than Mala's group. I liked Ida, but I still loved Mala.

When we reached sixth grade, our problems, attitudes, and conversations were slowly changing. A year ago, we were playing cops and robbers (*Ritter und Rauber*) or other children's games. Now, we frequently would just walk in groups and talk about movies, teachers, books, and homework. In my group, we talked a great deal about the Zionist organizations and their relative merits. We even talked and increasingly argued about politics, although as yet we knew very little about it.

Since we now were in the sixth grade, our homework was much more difficult. More often, students would remain in class during recess or before leaving school in order to discuss some of the more difficult assignments. It would be primarily students from the first group that actively participated in these conversations. However, since Ida joined our class, she would be there too with girls and boys from the middle group, including me. Mostly we tried to compare our school-work with hers to make sure we had it right. Up until then, Mala seldom—if ever—allowed one of us to compare or even look at her homework book, but Ida had no objections. Sometimes she even left her math book during recess so that we could compare or even copy it. I sometimes asked Richard if I could compare my homework with his, but he usually had already given his book to someone else from his group.

River Barges

My memories of school jolted to a halt when our Russian freight train reached the end of the railway line. We were in the city of Tyumen…in Siberia! Up to that time, I always thought of Siberia as being a forsaken, eternally cold place where criminals were sent; a big prison in a cold jungle. But Tyumen looked to me like any one of the many Russian cities and towns we saw from the train. It was July or August, and the weather was warm.

After we disembarked, we were taken to a *bania* (Russian bathhouse). It felt good to finally take a hot shower. It seemed strange to me that there were women attendants in the men's part of the bathhouse. It was awkward, to say the least, to be handed soap and a towel by a woman while I was naked. But they were very businesslike. There was a lot of nervous joking about it. Later on, we realized that in Soviet Russia, women work and do practically everything men do.

Staying in Tyumen was not the plan. We were taken to the river where there was a convoy of barges. The refugee army was loaded aboard these barges and again my family took care to remain together. We traveled farther into Siberia this way for more than several weeks, passing through the endless expanse of the *taiga* (forest and swampland). It all looked the same. Towns and camps along the bank were very rare. It was just an endless procession of trees and empty wilderness. As the rivers got smaller, some groups disembarked to work at local camps. Others, like us, were transferred to smaller barges. As I had done on the train journey, I passed the time recalling my school days. Thinking about my companions and my old life brought a kind of comfort to me, like a warm coat against the empty chill of the wilderness we traveled through.

11

Public School

We had four *gymnasium*s in our city. One was a business-oriented *gymnasium* with separate classes for boys and girls, where math and accounting were the primary subjects. The others were academic *gymnasium*s: two for boys and one for girls. These were for students who planned to go on to the university.

For admittance to a *gymnasium*, you had to pass a difficult, two-day entry examination. There were always many more applicants than there were spaces available. Also, at that time, anti-Semitism in our city was sharply on the rise and for a Jew to get into a *gymnasium* was made even more difficult. Hitler's anti-Semitic propaganda was spreading effectively at least in Poland and especially in Chorzow, where perhaps sixty percent of the people were Germans or Silesians who always sympathized with Germany. By now, our city's population was divided into two distinct groups: the old Upper Silesians and the recently arrived Poles. There was a great deal of animosity between the groups. Most jobs in the city administration, post office, and other important institutions were now given to these new arrivals from Poland. They were called by the derogatory term of *gorolu*. Even though I never heard adults use that expression, the fact their kids used it confirmed what they learned at home from their parents. It was obvious the Upper Silesians did not like the newcomers, but they could not do anything about it. So, they vented their frustrations against the Jews, especially those newly arrived Polish Jews. Logically, there should be nothing wrong with the word Jew or being called Jew when you are Jewish. But it was used as an insult, as if to say "You are bad and not my equal." Frequently some demeaning adjective was used with it, like "cursed Jew." Verbal expressions and graffiti on some buildings were gradually changing from profanities to *przeklenty Zydy* (cursed Jews).

Being accosted by gangs of Gentile boys began happening more frequently on our way to or from school. We tried to get out of their way and run, but sometimes we had to absorb a beating. In the past this happened mostly on a few really bad streets that could be avoided. But now it could happen on any street whenever we encountered a group of kids.

I always felt fairly safe on our street. But then I noticed that when a Jewish boy from another street passed, he too occasionally would be harassed, "Zyd, Zyd!" Some of the local kids would sometimes chase him. It bothered me that they would do it even when they knew I could see. Gradually I began to realize that, indirectly, they were reminding me that I too am different, lower than they were because I am a Jew. I no longer felt the same when playing with those kids, and I gradually stopped.

When I reached sixth grade, it was time to decide if I should apply for *gymnasium*. Richard and all his friends applied, and a great number of boys from my group did as well. The year was 1935 and, financially, times were not so good for my family. My mother was determined I go to *gymnasium*. Even though my father wanted it too, he frequently questioned if I would not be better off learning a trade. He was concerned we might not be able to afford *gymnasium*. Eventually my parents decided to register me, but then we learned I was too young. The fact that I had completed six years of public school did not matter.

My mother spoke to the principal of the Jewish public school to see if he could help, but he made it clear that under the best circumstances for a Jew to get into the *gymnasium* was difficult enough. In my case, it was really not even worth trying. I would have to continue on to seventh grade in the public school. I believe my father was relieved. It at least postponed the problem for a year, and he hoped our financial position might improve.

Mala and Richard applied to the academic *gymnasiums*. Richard applied to the one located in the center of the city on Ulica Powstancow, which was well-known for its outstanding professorial staff. We called it The Bude. It was also known to be rather anti-Semitic with very few Jews attending. The other one was located on Ulica Piotrkowska, on the western outskirts of the city and was known to have less stringent entry examinations. Although you could choose any one of the two, most students registered with the one nearest to their home. However, a few weeks before the examination, some of the students who applied to The Bude were notified that, because of the excessive number of applicants, they were transferred to the western *gymnasium*. They would have to take the examination there. All the Jewish applicants, including Richard, were transferred. Richard and about ten other Jewish students passed the examinations and were accepted to the western *gymnasium*.

I finished sixth grade and received a fairly good report card. It is true I studied more, but it is also true the teachers in the last year of the Jewish public school gave better grades to everyone. They didn't have to be told the difficulties we would be facing as Jews.

That summer, we went to Rabka Zdroj, a resort in the Karpaty Mountains. Usually our whole family, except my father, would go. But that summer everyone stayed to work. Only Moniek and I went, with my sister Lisa with her son Felix, who was one year old.

When we returned from the vacation and checked with the director of the Jewish public school, we found out I had been assigned to the public school located on Ulica Dombrowskiego. Manfred Wiener, another student from my sixth grade class, was also assigned there. Manfred was a much better student than I was. We had hardly ever spoken together. However, when we learned we would be going to the same new school together, we became friends. We decided to go register at the same time in order to ask to be assigned to the same classroom. We were granted this request, so we both felt a little better about going to the new school.

The school was in a rather large, four-story building about 300 meters long. It was much bigger than our old school. The classrooms were large, nice, and clean and so were the corridors. There was no comparison with the Jewish public school, which was in an old, deteriorated building. I realized the Jewish schools simply did not get their fair share of the public funding for schools. On our first day, it took us some time to find our classroom.

When Manfred and I got there, all the other students were already seated. We gave our registration slips to the teacher. He sat down behind his desk and pulled out a large book. In the silence of the big classroom, he began perusing the book.

We stood there awkwardly, knowing everyone in the class was looking at us. Not daring to look back, we kept our eyes on the teacher. He was less than six feet tall with a medium build, and around thirty-five years old with a small, black mustache and eyeglasses. He looked like a typical Upper Silesian. Somehow, we did not feel threatened by him, but nevertheless my heart kept pounding.

He peered again at Manfred's registration slip and said, "Manfred Wiener, date of birth?"

Manfred told him.

But now we could hear murmurs in the classroom and it was not difficult to distinguish the word *Zyd*.

Then the teacher asked, "Religion?"

"*Zyd*," Manfred stated.

Both our faces blushed red. The teacher then turned to me and asked the same questions. All this only took a few seconds. But, to us, it felt like eternity. We were both relieved when the teacher finally told us to take a seat. With great relief, we went to the only empty desk, far at the back of the classroom. As we walked down the long aisle, I felt like a sheep walking among the wolves. When we finally reached the sanctuary of the desk, we both took a deep breath. Only then did we scan around the faces in the classroom. Neither Manfred nor I knew anyone in the class.

The teacher, Mr. Mandel, taught music and gymnastics. He had an easygoing, friendly manner. We could easily see he was not one of those strict teachers that students usually fear.

It was not long before we got into a conversation with some of the students sitting nearby. They were friendly enough. They told us about the different teachers, specifically which were strict and which were lenient. We began to be much more at ease, but, in the schoolyard during recess, someone passing would then point at us and say "*Zyd.*"

Manfred and I made sure to stay together during recess, but soon realized we were very vulnerable to someone who wanted to provoke a fight. We decided always to stay close to the teacher on duty in the schoolyard, reasoning that no one would dare to start anything when a teacher was nearby. That was how we got by the first few days in school.

As days passed by, we made more acquaintances. I made sure I studied and did my homework diligently. Even though in the Jewish school I definitely was not one of the better students, here I had two good reasons to study. The first was the fact that it was much easier to make friends when you are a good student and can help others during recess. We would gladly let them compare homework. The second was that we feared the teachers and what they may do, especially if they turned out to be anti-Semites.

As time went on, we became friendly with as many students in our classroom as we possibly could, but also found some that obviously did not like us just because we were Jewish. The idea was that if we were friendly with someone, we didn't have to worry that he would harass us or start a fight. Fortunately, there were only two or three in our classroom that we knew were anti-Semites. And they would not dare to start anything in the classroom, or when we were in the company of other students, or near a teacher. But we still had the problem during recess in the schoolyard, in the corridors, and on the way to and from school. We noticed that in the schoolyard most of those kids that seemed to harass us and were itching for a fight were from other classes. They behaved like a street gang. They spent a great deal of time playing or just roaming around in groups, and they frequently used foul language.

Each of these gangs had a leader. He usually was the strongest and most daring and the bully of the group. The rest were usually *Nachschlepper* (tagalongs) who tried showing off to impress their leader. The difference was that the leader was usually physically strong, daring the tagalongs who were usually cowards who would not dare to do those things when they were alone. It was those tagalongs that would usually harass us. We were tempted to respond and would probably beat them, but we had to grit our teeth and resist the temptation. We knew, if we got into a fight with one, the others would most likely join in and we wouldn't stand a chance. We realized the only way to solve this problem was to get friendly with one of those group leaders, preferably one from a larger group. This would keep their group as well as the others off our back. But it was not that easy. Even though we were fairly friendly with one of those group leaders from our class, we recognized this group had relatively little influence outside the classroom. Anyway, we could not count on them to actively help us. The only way to get closer with those big boys was through sports, including soccer, handball, volleyball, and dodgeball.

Up until now, sports were just something I played when I had nothing else to do. It was definitely not something I gave much effort to. But whenever I did play, I seemed to be fairly good. My favorite sport was a game called *walka narodow* (battle of nations), or dodgeball.

The teacher appointed the two opposing team leaders and they in turn picked their teams. I was always one of the first picked because I was very good at avoiding being hit. In particular, I was known for catching the balls, which was considered a difficult, courageous thing to do.

Most of the games were played after school hours when we competed with other classes. Even though I was never selected as a leader of a team, there were occasions when I was one of the last players left on our team.

As the opposing team tried to knock me out, my teammates shouted encouragement, "Don't give in, Eichel!"

When I managed to catch a very hard throw, they would jump up and shout, "Eichel! Well done!"

When our team won an important game with another class, our classmates would practically lift us up and carry us around in jubilation. In this way, I became known throughout the school.

Soccer was the most popular sport in the city. Manfred was considered to be one of the best soccer players in the school. I was not that good in soccer, but I always went along with Manfred and I played occasionally. As time went on, I got better at it, and I was picked more frequently. I played left defense because I was a *kikut* (left leg kicker). Occasionally we played against a team from the other school. During those games, Manfred and I managed to get friendly with some of the "big boys" of the other school too.

Manfred and I always tried to hang around with some of those boys that were now friendly with us. This made it less likely that someone would harass us. By this time, we now felt fairly safe in the school, but still had some problems going to and from school. Here also, we tried not to walk alone. However, there were still occasions when I had to run to avoid a beating.

Twice a week, we had to attend the Jewish religious instruction our rabbi gave for all students in non-Jewish schools. It was held in the *gymnasium* located in the center of the city. There, we had a chance to meet all the other Jewish students and hear how they were managing. Most of them had similar problems we had, but had learned to somehow avoid serious fights. There were some however who were not as lucky. One of them was Perlmuter, a classmate from the Jewish school who was attending a school near ours; the only Jew. He complained that he has been assaulted a number of times in the schoolyard. He was taller than most of the students in our class and on the husky side. Because of his size, I would think nobody would want to pick a fight with him. But we knew him to be an *Angsthase* (fearful), or what we would call chicken. He always ran away from a fight.

I remember an incident from the time when we were still in the Jewish school. A group of us, including Perlmuter, was going home from school and saw a gang of four boys standing nearby. We continued walking, feeling they would not dare start anything. If they did, we agreed to fight if necessary. As we expected, they did not even look at us when we were passing them, but we realized that Perlmuter had deserted us. We counted on him being taller and stronger than any one of us, and we were disappointed he left us.

The situation in the school was different from the street because there was no place to run. Once you were recognized as being scared, it was over. The more aggressive boys would never leave you alone. Some of the boys who picked a fight with him were smaller and definitely not as strong, but they were trying to show off in front of their friends. Instead of fighting back, poor Perlmuter would cry and try to run away.

Since entering seventh grade in the Christian school, I studied more and had less time to spend in Betar. In the past, I always attended all the meetings, now I missed most of them except on Sunday. Since I left the Jewish school, I also lost contact with my school friends and only from time to time visited Richard. He was always with some of his friends. I was hoping to become friendly with them, but I realized, now that they were in *gymnasium* and I was still in public school, this was even less likely than before. I wanted to attend *gymnasium* too.

Around this time, my parents agreed to register me in the business *gymnasium*. I was pretty good in math and at least after I finished that *gymnasium*, I would at least be able to get a job as a bookkeeper. But once again, we were told I was too young. Then my mother wanted to register me for the academic *gymnasium*. My father, however, felt that unless you were ready to continue with education into the university, it did not make sense to go to academic *gymnasium*, something we most likely couldn't afford. Besides that, everyone knew that for a Jew to get into *gymnasium* was very difficult, and to get into a university was almost impossible. And you needed lots of money. He thought the business *gymnasium* was best, even if we had to wait another year. I also preferred the business *gymnasium* because I feared the exams in the academic *gymnasium*, where Polish language, which I considered my weakness, was very important. Eventually my mother agreed, and I continued onto the eighth grade in the same school.

It was a bad year for us, financially. For the first time, we spent the vacation at home. Only Salo went to the mountains for a weekend to visit his girlfriend Bella. The first week or two before Richard left for vacation, I visited him almost daily. He always had some friends there and they usually went for a walk in the park, and I would tag along. Richard was an exceptionally nice person. He knew his friends did not care much about me joining them, and he also knew that I would very much like to be in their company and he tried to accommodate me.

Since most of my friends were away on vacation, I was bored most of the time. I no longer cared to play with the boys on the street, and Horst was more interested in chasing the girls than playing with me. I spent more time in Betar playing Ping-Pong. That year, Mala Ringelheim came back from vacation early and inflamed my interest again. But now that she was going to the girls' *gymnasium*, there was hardly any pretext I could find to approach her.

One day, I noticed Mala's younger brother, Wolek, playing on the street. It occurred to me that he might be useful to me in getting closer to Mala. He was one year younger than I was and belonged to Betar as well. I made it a point to become friendly with him, playing Ping-Pong and even walking back home because he lived across the street from us. Before long, he invited me up to his place to play Ping-Pong. The Ringelheims' apartment was smaller than ours: only one room and a kitchen. They had a large dining room table and we positioned two chairs on each side of the table and then tied a long scarf across to serve as the net. I was surprised his mother had no objections to this. When I suggested it to my mother, I got a short, firm answer, "Absolutely not."

Ping-Pong was very popular among Jewish kids. It was played in all-Zionist organizations, and there was always a long waiting line for the table. That was why we frequently played in his apartment. Sometimes, when Mala was home, she would join us. I would be in seventh heaven. We would talk, even if it was only about Ping-Pong.

On one hand, I was satisfied to be friendly with Wolek. It frequently provided an opportunity for me to see Mala and sometimes even talk to her. On the other hand, I was not happy about it because Wolek was younger, and Mala considered him and his friends as children. She never spoke to me about anything personal, the way she would speak to someone she regarded as a peer. She considered me as only a friend to her younger brother.

Occasionally, while I was in their house with Wolek, Mala's girlfriends came to visit her. When they saw me, Mala always explained I was playing with her little brother. That was embarrassing to me. Only a year ago, they were my classmates, and I now appeared to them to be acting like a younger kid.

I repeatedly promised myself to stop my relationship with Wolek. However, after a few days, I would again talk to him and visit his house, just to be close to Mala. The more I kept on doing this, the more I felt ashamed. Love had me going back and forth like a Ping-Pong ball.

12

Sojma

Thoughts of Mala played in my mind while my eyes stared blankly at the endless procession, day after day, of trees and more trees along the endless bank of the river while our barge moved slowly deeper into Siberia. The only change was that the river gradually grew narrower.

Then we ran aground, or so I thought. The Russians who operated the barge acted as if this were planned, but there was nothing about the place that would make anyone think it was a destination. It was just more trees, identical to the ones we had been passing for the last thousand kilometers. Then some uniformed officers appeared out of the woods. The bargemen put a plank to the shore and helped us as we disembarked.

We didn't know it at the time, but we were literally in the middle of Siberia; about 1,000 kilometers north of the city of Omsk. We had begun on the Ob River, the largest in Russia. We then went to the Irtish and lastly to the Sojma River, which was no more than fifty feet wide when we stopped.

The soldiers led us up a path in through dense forest for a few hundred feet. Behind us, we could hear the barges heading back down river. We came to a clearing with some wooden buildings around it, the center of the camp. We assembled there, numbering about 300. A handful of Russian officers waited patiently for everyone to get to the clearing.

One of them stepped forward and introduced himself as Officer Obryskov of the NKVD, the Soviet Security Forces. Obryskov was six feet tall and wore a tailored uniform with epaulets.

"You have been designated as Special Resettlers," he said. "You will live and work in this camp, Sojma, under the supervision of the NKVD. The work available here is cutting down trees. We will have Russians from nearby settlements show you how to do it. You will get paid for your work, based on production."

Someone from our group raised his hand. "We do not mind working," he said. "But most of us are from different professions. We prefer to work in our own trades."

"What is your profession?" asked Obryskov.

"I was working in the bank," the man said.

Other people shouted, "Plumber...Shoemaker...Teacher...Lawyer."

Obryskov raised his arm. "For those of you who did not notice," he said, "we are in the middle of the *taiga* here. We do not need plumbers and shoemakers. We need to cut down trees. That is all that is available for you." In a firmer voice, he then added, "And we have a law in our country. He who does not work, does not eat."

As serious as he sounded, we really did not take it that way. We still were convinced we were only there on a temporary basis.

Someone from the crowd shouted, "As soon as the war is over, we will go back to our hometowns anyway."

Obryskov scanned the group for a long moment. "As you cannot see the earlobe of your ear," he said, "so will you never see your hometown."

He turned away for a moment and spoke to an officer next to him. Obryskov gestured toward the officer, a stocky man with a smiling disposition. "This is Tovarish Koltunov, the commandant in charge of this camp," Obryskov said. "He will explain to you in detail what is going to happen now."

The commandant pointed in the direction of three wooden buildings at the edge of the clearing. "These are your living quarters," he said. "In a while, we will call out the names of the people assigned to each of these barracks. Tonight and for the next two days, you will be served free breakfast, lunch, and supper in the *stolovaja* (dining hall)." He pointed to a building on the opposite side of the clearing.

He continued to explain that we also would be given a daily ration of bread, a half-pound per person. After two days, we would be required to pay for our food. He suggested we use the two days to become settled and clean up around the barracks. He declared we were not allowed to leave the camp without his permission and warned us not to stray too far because we might get lost in the woods or swamps. He also informed us that we would be able to buy clothing and other goods in the store located in the same building as the *stolovaja*.

A deputy then read a list of names assigning people to one of the three barracks. Soon, on the list for the first building, he called out, "Abram Leibowicz Eichel, Alexander Abramowicz, Joseph Abramowicz, and Simon Abramowicz."

And so, from then on, I was Simon Abramowitch; Simon, son of Abram. We stopped speaking German at Sojma, even among ourselves. I was no longer called Siegfried.

After our names were called, we immediately went to the barracks. It was a rectangular log cabin, about sixty feet long and thirty feet wide. A single door was in the middle. Only a small window was on each long side of the building.

There were two rows of shelves, about seven feet wide, running along the walls, interrupted only by the windows. The bottom shelf was about a foot above the floor. The higher shelf was about four feet above that. These would serve as our bunks for sleeping. In the middle of the room was a cast iron stove with the pipe running straight up through the roof. In front of that was a long wooden table with benches. We were among the first to arrive in the barracks. After a quick survey of the room, my father told us to take places on the higher shelf. We climbed up to claim our space, putting down our knapsacks and bags.

Sometimes the pivotal moments of a lifetime come from a decision or action we take. That's understandable; there's some element of control in that. But sometimes these moments just happen—an accident—and you forever ask yourself why. You replay the moments in your mind a thousand times as if, by an act of will, to try to make a different outcome. But we can't change what has already passed. Even today, I remember what happened when I was climbing up to the bunk in the barracks at Sojma. It still makes me cringe.

In our knapsack, we had a bottle of vodka Salo had received from the Hellers in Lvov; a precious commodity. As I was climbing up the ladder to the top bunk, I inadvertently grabbed the sack from the bottom. The bottle fell to the floor. It smashed in a fragrant pool, the dark liquid on the wooden floor, the glittering shards of broken glass. I gaped in horror. To lose such a priceless luxury—it still makes me cringe. Salo had cared for it and prized it and schlepped it all the way from Lvov.

If there ever was a time in my life that I felt I deserved the worst, that was it. My self-esteem shrank to microscopic dimensions. Throughout the cold winter that was to follow I was reminded, a thousand times, how good it would have been to have just a small sip of that warming vodka.

I hardly noticed as more people came in to the barracks and we had to squeeze our sleeping area tighter together. Eventually there were about 100 people. I don't think anyone had an inkling of how serious our predicament was or the hardships that lie ahead. I think most of us felt, compared to the overt threat posed by the Germans, the Russians were not much more than a nuisance to be tolerated. We could even tease them. About six months after our arrival, we learned that Obryskov had died suddenly.

We teased the Russians at Sojma, "You better watch out, or the same thing will happen to you."

The local Russians were mostly *kulaks* (farmers) that Stalin had forcefully resettled to Siberia some fifteen years before. Some of them had built the camp at Sojma, and they had to vacate to make room for us. They now lived in a similar settlement called Basa about seven kilometers away. They did not tease the authorities. They knew from first-hand experience what the NKVD was capable of doing. We did not.

The building that housed the *stolovaja* also housed the bakery and a small store. The *stolovaja* was a single, large room with five long, wooden tables and benches. The large doorway to the kitchen was open, and you could see in. Some Russian men and women worked there. That was where we lined up to pick up our meals. The meal given to us that first day was one of which we would grow numbly familiar: a bowl of soup and a plate of either potatoes or oats. The soup, called *offsianka*, had more water than substance. My father said the grain floating in it was used in Europe to feed pigs. I don't think he was joking.

The next day, we visited the store. They sold articles of winter clothing, some tools, and even some candy, but very few food products. The prices were astronomical compared to Lvov. So were the prices on the very limited menu in the *stolovaja*. At first, we still had some money that we had earned in Lvov and, because we still believed that we would not be staying long, we didn't worry too much. We even bought a few pieces of candy.

The refugees in Sojma were mainly Jewish, but there were also some Christians from mid-Poland, a few couples from Czechoslovakia, and one young man in his early twenties from Vienna. We were the only people from Upper Silesia. The Polish Jews were predominantly from villages or smaller cities with large Jewish communities. But there were a few from Warsaw and one from the city of Lodz. There were two families with children, the Siegels and the Hochmans, but their children were older. I was the youngest at Sojma.

The day we reported to work, we were met by the Commandant Koltunov, his deputy, and a number of Russian civilians. We were divided into work groups of ten or fifteen men. Some groups also had women. Each group was assigned one of the Russians. My father, brothers, Hassenberg, and I were together in a group. Koltunov explained we would be paid for the work the group did on a weekly basis. Everybody was issued an ax, which looked more like a hatchet with a slightly curved, short handle. We were told we were personally responsible for this tool and if we lost it we would have to pay for a replacement. Each group also received a few five-foot handsaws with handles on each end.

Following our Russian foreman, we marched into the woods. There were swamps all around us. We walked about two kilometers before we stopped. The foreman selected a tree and showed us how to cut it down. The tree he picked was at least two feet wide at the base. He used his ax to cut a notch in the tree about a foot above ground. He explained the notch had to be just big enough to make the tree fall. He then made a wedge from a piece of wood he found nearby and knocked it into the notch. This helped the tree fall in the direction he wanted. He did that very quickly and made it look easy. However, when I started to do it, I found it was a lot harder than it looked. I had a problem simply hitting the exact spot on the tree repeatedly, and I didn't know when to start knocking in the wedge.

After a few days, some of us in the group, including Josel and I, learned how to do it fairly well ourselves. Salo and Hassenberg were pretty clumsy and really never learned. We would not allow my father to even try.

We may have not realized it at the time, but a certain hierarchy had formed in our family. When it came to physical strength, there was no doubt that Josel and I had the distinction, not only in the family but in the entire camp. Salo was considered the most educated, well-spoken, and refined. My father, of course, was indisputably the wisest, our unquestioned leader. Being the youngest, I was considered the kid. As such, I had a unique, protective atmosphere around me. Josel, since that incident in Chorzow working with the Nazis, was renowned for having guts. We never discussed this hierarchy among ourselves. It was simply understood.

I once overheard Hassenberg say to my father, "You are keeping your sons together on a very tight leash. You are very strict with them."

"If we stick together," my father said, "we will survive. I want to make sure we all survive."

Since joining us in the police station in Lvov, Hassenberg became a de facto member of our family. We all accepted him, but not necessarily because we liked him. Many times, it was just the opposite. He was clumsy, not strong, and had many characteristics we didn't like. He was annoying in being super-thrifty and smugly self-disciplined. And he had a leisurely attitude about everything that could be maddening.

Sometimes Josel was partnered with Hassenberg using the long saw to cut a felled tree into logs. Hassenberg pulled his side of the saw very slowly and would not match Josel's pace.

Finally, Josel would blurt out, "Hassenberg! For God's sake, pull faster!"

Hassenberg stopped sawing altogether and regarded his unhappy partner. "Josel," he said. "You pull your side the way you want, and I'll pull my side the way I want."

Josel could only throw up his hands in exasperation.

Or when we were in the *stolovaja*, he would ask Josel or me, "Can you lend me a kopek? I need a little more for the soup."

We would give it to him, not knowing that he just borrowed from my father or Salo. Of course, we caught on eventually.

Despite these things, my father insisted he be treated like family. After all, he was the only relative we had in the place. And we never disputed our father's authority. We may not have liked it, but we always obeyed.

In retrospect, I am convinced my father's answer to Hassenberg about our survival together was undeniably true. We saw many families, couples, and siblings break up and live miserably afterward—or even perish. If separated, each of us would have suffered much more than we actually did. But we were stronger because we were together. And we stayed together because of the leadership of my father. Up until today, I frequently wonder if I have even come close to the wisdom and leadership of my father. Often I doubt it. I guess this will be up to my children to decide for themselves.

After we felled a tree, we chopped off all the branches. Then, some of the tall, straight trees were set aside for structural timber. Most of the logs were cut and stacked into neat piles about ten feet long. At the end of each day, a Russian inspector would measure the stacks and mark a number of logs with chalk. At the end of the week, we would be paid based on the number of cubic meters the group cut.

After the first full week of work, our group received enough pay to buy a day's worth of food at the *stolovaja*. We joked about this and continued to treat the work more like play. In many groups, people found excuses to skip work completely. However, as time went on, the money ran low, and everyone began to take work seriously. The younger, single people formed their own work groups. Some of the older men and women formed cleanup crews. Also, other jobs were gradually created as we replaced the Russians working in the kitchen, bakery, and store.

When we started work at Sojma, it was the end of August 1940. Back home, the Polish town of Oswiecim, about thirty kilometers from our home in Chorzow, had been renamed Auschwitz by the Germans. They opened a brand new facility there for the extermination of Jews and other undesirables.

In Siberia, the weather had started turning cooler. Then it turned colder and colder, beyond our experience. Our clothing was no longer adequate. We had to buy warmer underwear, shirts, and *kufaika* (heavily quilted work coats and pants). *Kufaika* was warm, but it was very, very expensive. That dramatically changed the financial condition not only for us, but for everybody else in the camp. Everybody became much more dependent on the income from work. We found out from some of the Russians working with us that most prices they paid were lower than ours. They too were classified as Special Resettlers and so should have been under the same restrictions as we. They were much more fearful of the authorities and hardly ever complained. But we went straight to Commandant Koltunov and complained about the prices. After that, some of the basic food prices were reduced. The NKVD knew, that while we had money, we would be reluctant to work. They gave our store a much greater selection of goods than they had at the Russian Basa camp—or so we were told—but those goods were priced very high.

The Siberian winter descended with endless snowfall and temperatures sometimes passing forty below zero. I always liked winter at home. We used to play in the snow, go sled riding, build snowmen, and have snowball fights. I don't know how many inches of snow fell in Chorzow a year, maybe ten or fifteen. That amount did not inconvenience us very much. The schools and all the stores stayed open.

But in Siberia when it snows, you measure it in feet, not inches. When the first snow came, I was very happy to see it. I guess I was still a kid at heart. But it seemed to snow forever. When it finally stopped and we walked out of the barracks, we were knee deep in it. It was very hard to walk, but still we had to go to work. We soon learned to follow previous footprints and after a while, we learned the cardinal rule of staying on the path, whatever it might be. Hassenberg once decided to take a shortcut, and he wound up falling into snow up to his chin. We had to rescue him. His head seemed disembodied there on the surface of the snow as he squawked for help.

The real problem was the severe cold. Even though we were bundled into *kufaika* as well as multiple layers of underwear and shirts and felt snow boots called *valinkis*, we were still freezing cold. When it's like that, you want to just curl up into a ball and stick your hands under your arms. If it was not for my father, we would have surely frozen to death. Some people did.

My father would frequently scream at us, "Keep moving! Work faster! Don't stay still, or you will freeze to death."

We soon learned three places on the face are vulnerable to freezing—ears, cheeks, and nose. They could suddenly turn white with frostbite, and you would not even feel it. At first, this made us panic. Then the Russians taught us to rub snow on the frozen area. After that, we made a regular practice of frequently scanning each other's faces. Someone would say to you "right cheek" or "left ear." You then rubbed in some snow and continued to work.

In the winter, we couldn't cut trees, so we moved the ones we had previously cut. We stacked the logs on a crude, horse-drawn sled. The horse dragged it through the snow down to the frozen river. There, we loaded the logs on to rafts that sat on the ice. At first, the Russians handled the horses and built the rafts. Later on, we learned to do those things too. I was never comfortable handling the horses. I guess I'm a city boy at heart.

We used the family whistle frequently at work when one of us needed a hand with something or when it was time to quit work and walk back to the barracks. Occasionally our friends used to imitate the whistle, but we in the family could always recognize each other's call.

In the winter, the food problem was worse. Hardly anything edible, except mushrooms and some very bitter berries, grew in Siberia. All food had to be imported from the south. The only way for us to get food was through the *stolovaja* or the store. But all you could buy in the store was some varieties of oats and bread.

The bread was black and looked like pumpernickel but was even denser. The half-pound ration (so small!) was distributed in the evening. Each barrack received its share of bread, which then had to be cut into rations. The occupants of each barrack appointed a committee of three to make sure the total barrack's allotment of bread was picked up from the store everyday, divided, and distributed fairly. Salo was on the committee and was frequently asked to cut the bread. This was not an easy job with every critical eye watching.

Josel and I always ate our ration the moment we got it. He and I were continually hungry. Even though my father advised us to save some for tomorrow, we could not. By eleven o'clock, we grew hungry to the point where we were sometimes too weak to work. We counted the long minutes until lunch. I could never understand why my father and Salo were not hungry. Maybe they were, but didn't show it.

One day while I was walking with Josel, I complained, "Josel, I am so hungry."

"I'm hungry, too," he said.

He looked at the expression of misery on my face and said "When we get home, the first thing I'll tell mother will be to use her largest pot…" He paused to see that he had my full attention. "And I'll tell her to put in the best cut of meat. And the best cut of fish…"

"You can't cook meat and fish together," I said, taking his bait. He only wanted to distract me and make me forget my hunger.

"Why not?" he challenged. "Both are good things."

"So tell her to put in the best chocolate, too." So we would have long, academic discussions about food. Our bodies may have been trudging through the frozen snows of Siberia, bellies empty, but, in our minds, we were standing in our warm kitchen in Chorzow, luxuriating in the fragrance of the imagined meal on the table, and we could taste it.

Hunger does more than make your imagination vivid. It defies the mind and makes you compromise your moral behavior.

One night, we were lying down to sleep. My father, Salo, and Hassenberg were already fast asleep when Josel nudged me.

"Look what's in Hassenberg's coat pocket," he whispered.

When my eyes saw, my hand moved and took out of his pocket Hassenberg's ration of bread from the previous evening. He had not touched it.

Josel took out his knife and looked at me. I nodded my approval. Josel cut two thin slices, and then gently put the remaining bread back into Hassenberg's pocket. I cannot confess that my conscience was troubled by this. The bread melted in my mouth in an instant and then I slept deeply.

The following morning, we heard Hassenberg complaining to my father about his bread. He suspected Josel. They even consulted Salo to confirm that the portion looked smaller.

Later my father cornered Josel and me out of earshot of anyone else. "Did you take Hassenberg's bread?" he demanded.

We swore we did not, but our father knew our eyes.

Under a furrowed brow, his gaze burned into our faces. "Stealing bread from one of us here is not only stealing. It is murder." He stared at us a moment more. "Don't ever do it!" he hissed, then turned abruptly and walked away from us.

13

Examinations

At Sojma, I began writing about my life in a notebook. It was something I did only to pass the time. Also I guess it helped me remember that I had a life beyond the Siberian wilderness. I wrote mostly about my school experiences.

Around the middle of my year in eighth grade, we again had to decide how I would proceed to get into a *gymnasium*. My first choice was the business *gymnasium*. My mother went to register me for the entrance examination, but she found there were no more openings. My old classmate Ida Brecher was accepted there the previous year and she was the only Jewish student to make it out of fifteen applicants.

We decided I would try for The Bude. That was the most difficult one, but it was on Ulica Powstancow, only about four blocks from my house. It was also the most expensive, and our family was not having a good year, financially. Richard had tried to take the exams there, but he was diverted to the other *gymnasium* on Ulica Piotrkowska. That was where he was attending, along with many other Jewish students. Perhaps I too would be diverted there. That was fine with me. I would like to be with Richard, even though the school was at least a half hour walk from our house. That would present a challenge in avoiding the street gangs in warm weather and the cold of winter too.

My mother was able to register me for the exams at The Bude. The exams would take place immediately after the school year, only five months away. At first, I was afraid. Richard and all my other friends had been unable to get into this *gymnasium*. How could I expect to get in?

Then I felt a kind of grim determination. I was in my last year of public school. If I did not get into *gymnasium*, I would have to learn a trade while all the people I wanted to be friends with were wearing the uniform of the *gymnasium*. I would have to find a new group of non-student friends and forget about Richard and his group. That was something I certainly wanted to avoid.

To help me prepare for the examinations, my father hired Professor Sprecher to tutor me. Professor Sprecher was the only Jewish professor at The Bude. He was well-known for his work in mathematics and was well-respected and influential. I began working with the professor, and I studied hard. Never had I been so motivated. Aside from wanting badly to be in Richard's group, I knew failing the exam would cause a great deal of embarrassment to my family and to me personally. I was very much afraid of suffering that embarrassment, and that fear gave me the strength to study hard.

Polish was my weak point. My mother then decreed Polish to be the official language of our household to help me improve.

With this new goal ahead of me, my life changed completely and my contact with the outside world diminished. For an hour after school, five days a week, I worked with Professor Sprecher. The rest of the day and weekends, I would study and study and study. I met Wolek occasionally on the street, but only exchanged a few words with him. I even found myself thinking less about Mala. My work at school was going well too, since I was now so much in the habit of studying. Although I stopped participating in after-school sports, I kept up my friendships and maintained my good standing among my classmates.

On weekends, I frequently visited Richard and always had good conversation. He frequently gave me advice about the examinations. Sometimes he posed questions that I might be asked. He helped me with the answers if needed and suggested books for me to read. The very best thing, though, was his frequent assurances that I was doing fine and did not need to worry. He really helped build my confidence.

However, I did still worry, in particular about my Polish grammar and composition. I regretted what I missed in the first six years in public school when playing was more important to me than studying. Getting a "C," a passing grade, was the only thing I cared about. All my subjects, except Polish, required only hard work for me to overcome my shortcomings. But learning the Polish language additionally required a feel and a good ear for detecting what was right or wrong. That only came with time, and I did not have much time. In my mind, I would think in German and then translate into Polish. Richard assured me I was improving and that my Polish was fine. Still, this was the subject I studied hardest.

The day before the examinations were to be held, I went to school as usual, preoccupied with the task ahead. My school day was interrupted with an announcement. All students who were to take entrance examinations to a *gymnasium* had to report to a designated classroom. We were to take a so-called "Intelligence Test."

There were about twenty other students in the classroom. The director of the school entered the room.

Distributing a twelve-page booklet, he said, "No one is to open the cover until I give a sign to start. The questions in this booklet are relatively easy and must be answered as quickly as you can. As soon as you are finished, you must immediately hand it in to me and I will note the exact time."

He further explained the booklets would be forwarded to the appropriate *gymnasium* and would have a significant bearing on whether we would be accepted or not. He cautioned, even though the questions were very easy, one could easily make a mistake if one was in too much of a hurry. Then he repeated that time was very important. He gave the sign to start.

He was right, the questions were easy.

"How much is two times six?"

"What is a person to you if she is the daughter of your mother's father?"

Some questions, although easy, were phrased in a tricky way, so on those I made myself slow down and read the question carefully.

I was not the very first one to finish, but I answered all the questions and turned in my booklet relatively fast. I was confident that I gave correct answers.

On June 20, 1936, I received my report cards and my diploma stating that I completed public school education. I was pleasantly surprised because my grades were even better than I expected. That was important since the report card had to be submitted to the *gymnasium*.

Examinations began the next day. My mother and sister Lisa accompanied me to the *gymnasium*. As we entered the building, my mother turned to me with great anxiety.

In Yiddish she said, "*Es soll sein mit mazel* (It should be with luck)."

I could feel her fear wash over me. As we entered the corridor, my heart started to pound hard enough to jump out from my body. It was hard to breathe.

There were a lot of people in the corridor, and it seemed hot and airless to me. We heard that there was a list posted on a bulletin board with names of students whose examinations had been transferred to the other *gymnasium*. This is what happened to Richard. We ran to the bulletin board and elbowed forward to read it. My eyes bore down the column of names. My name was not on it; that meant I could take the exam after all. I scanned the column again and saw again, with great relief, my name was not on it. However, of the thirty-five Jewish applicants, all but seven were transferred to the other *gymnasium*.

Another list was soon posted, indicating the classroom each student should report to. I was with the twin Spandorf brothers. We marched ahead to the room.

My mother and Lisa remained in the corridor and I went forward as if in a court-room, to meet my fate. I couldn't feel my feet on the floor or my legs moving. Except the Spandorfs, there was no one else in the room that I knew. I sat down behind them. I was not friends with them. They were a little younger than I was, and their parents were rich and respected. But I felt more comfortable with them since they were Jewish and I didn't know anyone else. As I looked around again, I saw other kids from the most prominent and richest families in Chorzow.

I could barely sit still, I was so nervous. The Spandorf brothers were normally boisterous, but they were now quiet as well. However, some of the other students in the room seemed to be without worry, running around the aisles and talking to each other. I found this completely inexplicable. Could they be that confident? How?

One of them was Zymirski, the son of the owner of the largest drugstore in the city. Observing his careless behavior, it suddenly occurred to me that maybe he had nothing to worry about. His father had probably fixed everything. For him, this was maybe just a formality—an annoyance. But for some of us, it was like life or death.

The door opened, and, the school director came in accompanied by a professor. Zymirski sat down. There was silence in the class.

The director cleared his voice as he coolly looked across the room. "The examination will take two days," he said. "On the third day, the results will be announced in the auditorium. Today, you will be given a written test in Polish language and mathematics. Tomorrow, you will have verbal questions for history, geography, and mathematics." He paused a moment and held up his hand for emphasis. His eyes seemed kind; he seemed to know how nervous we were. "Don't be in a hurry," he urged. "And write carefully. I wish you good luck." He left the room, and the professor addressed us.

"We will start with the Polish test," he said.

"Good," I thought. "Let's get the worst over with."

He began to distribute writing materials.

"I will write three subjects on the blackboard. Choose one. You have two hours to complete the written test. Write your full name on the top of the first page. Immediately below, write the title of the subject you choose. There will be no talking. Copying from someone else is forbidden. Anyone doing this will be immediately asked to leave the classroom and will be disqualified from the examination." His tone of voice had a bored drone to it, as if he had given thousands of these examinations. But we clung to every word.

"As soon as you finish, turn in the papers to me and you may then leave the class." He walked over to the blackboard and wrote the three subjects. "You may begin."

The room was so quiet for a moment that you could have heard a fly flying. Then came the sound of pencils scraping on paper. We had begun.

I calmed myself. "Siegfried," I said silently. "Think clearly now. Don't be nervous."

I studied the three options on the blackboard. I took my time deciding which one to choose. I don't remember the exact wording of the subjects, but two were about Polish history, and the third was a general theme. Even though I knew the first two subjects well, I chose the third. I reasoned that, on the first two, I would have to be doubly careful; not to make errors in Polish grammar and also to make sure of the historical facts. I chose the general theme so I would only need to concentrate on grammar and composition.

"Be cool," I said to myself. "Don't rush."

I began to write and my nervousness vanished completely. But it came back a little when I heard the first bell indicating that one hour had passed. I kept going. I got a little more nervous again when the first few students handed in their papers and left the classroom. By the time I finished my paper and reread it twice, there were only a few students left in the classroom.

I had reached the end of my ability to improve the paper, so I turned it in and walked toward the door. I had a flash of anxiety that maybe I should have checked it one more time. But now, it was too late. I left the room.

As I entered the hallway, my mother greeted me. "*Got zeid dank* (Thanks to God). Seeing so many students come out and not you," she said. "It really got me worried."

"So how did it go?" Lisa asked.

"I think I did fine, but I can't be sure."

"Do you think you made mistakes?" asked my mother.

I could see the anxiety in her face. I realized that the waiting had taken a toll on her. She must have been even more uneasy when she saw other students coming out, including the Spandorf twins.

I answered, "I just can't be sure."

I was instantly sorry that I didn't encourage her more. I only did it to leave myself an opening so if, God forbid, I failed, I would be able to say I knew it.

Lisa asked me to tell her in detail what I wrote. As I told her, she nodded and said, "That's good" or "That's right." Finally, she said, "Don't worry. You did well."

My mother breathed easier. She put her hand around my shoulder and squeezed me affectionately.

As we were walking around in the hallway before the next examination, my father arrived and brought me a piece of cake. It was an expensive cake that we seldom ate at home; a real treat for me. While I was eating, Lisa told him that it seemed I did all right. He looked around, took my mother aside a little, and spoke to her in a low voice.

"Look who is here. The elite from Chorzow. Zymirski, Hanke, and the Spandorfs. Do you think our son has a chance? A poor Jew? I don't think so."

He was almost whispering and did not intend for me to hear this. But I did. And I saw the anxiety return to my mother's face.

A little later, Richard came by. I was happy to see him. I told him in detail what I wrote. He also reassured me. He even asked me to spell some of the words I used. In every instance, he assured me it was correct. He sounded even more confident than my sister did, and he had experience with this kind of examination. So that gave me a real boost.

We were soon called back to the classroom for the math examination. Although Professor Sprecher was one of those giving the math exam, he was in one of the four or five other classrooms where the exams were being given.

The professor in my classroom spoke, "I will write the math problems on the blackboard in sequence. Copy one problem at a time, and write the answer next to it." Then he walked to the blackboard and wrote down the first problem. "You can start now."

He waited a moment while we copied the first problem and then proceeded to write the others. I had been a little nervous but when I saw the problems on the blackboard, I calmed down completely. They were sixth-grade problems, and I had completed the eighth grade.

Nevertheless, I checked and rechecked each answer carefully before going to the next problem. I noticed the student next to me, a boy I didn't know, was struggling and trying to see what I was doing. I made it easy for him to look at my papers, simply positioning them on the side of my desk in a way the professor could never notice.

The Spandorf twins, who were sitting in front of me, were having problems. They seemed almost unable to restrain themselves from turning fully around to look at my papers. From that angle, they could not be subtle like the student next to me, even though all my answers were underlined.

The student next to me had three more problems to work on. Even though I was finished, I waited a minute, allowing him to copy my answers before I got up to leave. I was the third one to turn in my papers and leave the classroom, but this time I had no anxiety. As I walked out I saw by the look on their faces that the Spandorfs were not doing so well.

My mother and Lisa were waiting for me in the corridor.

"Very good," I said to them before they could even ask. "Some of the problems were very easy."

My mother sighed with relief, a proud smile of satisfaction on her face.

As we walked back home, I told them about the boy sitting next to me and about the Spandorfs having problems. Maybe I was bragging a little, but, deep inside, I was still apprehensive, as if I didn't dare tempt fate by being cocky.

Before dinner, I tried to study history and geography, but I just couldn't concentrate. I guess I was too excited, or mentally exhausted, or just plain worried. I usually had no problems sleeping, but that night all kinds of crazy ideas popped into my head. What if I failed? What would I tell my friends? They would laugh at me. What profession would my father choose for me? Tailor? Somehow, that did not excite me much. What else could I do?

It seemed I had only just begun to doze off when my mother came into the room to wake me.

"It is time to get up," she said.

At first, I wondered how she could tease me like this in the middle of the night before my exams. Then I realized it really was morning.

Again my mother and Lisa went with me to school. I went to the same classroom and sat down in the same seat. The student next to me who I had helped greeted me with a smile.

"Hi! Listen," he said conspiratorially "thanks for helping me out yesterday."

We talked a bit. It was obvious he was quite nervous, like me.

Three professors came into the classroom. Two of them sat down at the desk in front of the room. The third one hung a large map of Europe on the blackboard and announced, "This is the geography verbal test. We will call out five names at a time in alphabetical order. Those students will come to the blackboard and will be asked questions one at a time. If you don't know the answer, just say so. After we are finished questioning you, you may leave the classroom and wait until the next hour of questioning starts."

They called the first five names. The professors at the desk pulled out notebooks and pencils and prepared to make notes. Since my name starts with E, I had to wait a little. As I listened to the questions, it was easy to see how nervous the students were in answering. My heart started thumping nervously, too. I tried to figure out which group of students I would be in, but I didn't know most of the names in the class, so it was impossible to predict.

The first questions pertained to locations of some countries and the names of their capitals. These questions were easy for me, but some of the students at the board had problems with some answers. If one student did not know or gave the wrong answer, the professor would ask the student next to him, "Do you know the answer?" or "Do you think this is right?"

I continued to be pretty nervous until I heard my name called. As I walked to the blackboard, I calmed down a little. But the boy standing next to me was so nervous that he was trembling.

The professor began to ask questions of the first student. I listened attentively as he answered all of them correctly. He was told he could leave the classroom, then the professor turned to the nervous boy next to me. Seeing how nervous the boy was, the professor smiled and tried to calm him down.

"Don't be afraid," he said. "We won't bite you." He waited a moment for the boy to compose himself and asked, "What country is southwest of France?"

The boy lowered his head to avoid looking at the professor. He had stopped shaking, but was perhaps simply unable to think. I was glad he stopped shaking. It was making me nervous, too.

The professor gently repeated, "What country is southwest of France? Do you know the answer?"

The boy was too beside himself to even be aware that we were standing next to a map of Europe. He didn't even need to turn his head to see France. The professor had clearly given him the easiest question possible to help him relax, but it didn't work.

Finally, the boy quietly mumbled, "The Mediterranean?"

"Now, calm down, and think it over. What country is southwest of France?" he repeated, this time putting emphasis on the word "country." He waited another moment and then turned to me. "Do you know what country is southwest of France?'

"Spain."

He then proceeded to ask other questions—each a little more difficult—about names of mountain ranges and rivers in various countries. I had no problems answering them. I was told I could leave the classroom and, as I walked out, it occurred to me to be thankful to Professor Sprecher who had prepared me so well. Many of the questions I had just answered were ones he specifically had me study.

In the corridor, the concerned faces of my mother and Lisa disappeared when they saw me smiling.

"So everything must have gone well?" asked Lisa.

"Yes, I think so." A shadow of doubt passed across my mother's face. "Yes, yes, it went very well," I said. I could see this waiting was really hard for my mother. I felt sorry for her.

Mrs. Spandorf came over to us and asked me how her boys were doing. I explained to her they were questioning students in alphabetical order and it would be a while until they got to "S." Mrs. Spandorf continued chatting with Lisa, and I tried calming my mother.

Finally, one of the Spandorf twins came out.

He was smiling and almost shouted, "I answered all the questions right!"

His mother was elated. As she tried to ask him about his brother, the classroom door opened and the brother was there, beaming.

He ran toward his mother. "Mom! Mom! I did well. I answered all the questions. It was easy."

Mrs. Spandorf finished hugging her kids. After they calmed down a bit, my mother asked the boys how I did.

"Siegfried did great," they said. "He got every one right." Finally relieved, she turned to me and kissed me on my forehead and hugged me. It felt good, and I was happy that my mother was happy.

Salo showed up while we waited for the next session to begin. He explained that my father needed Lisa in the store, so she wished me luck and left. Salo said he would remain with my mother. When Lisa left, Salo asked me how it went with the exam. I said fine, and he patted my shoulder. Then he began chatting with Mrs. Spandorf. I know Salo wanted me to do well, but his interest was not as warm or welcome as Lisa's was.

The bell rang, and we returned to the classroom for the final examination. Three professors again entered. One was the same professor that gave the written math test. He brought those tests along with him and placed them on the desk.

He took up one of the papers and then called out the name, asking the student to come to the blackboard. It soon became evident that this portion was not in alphabetical order. He then dictated a mathematical problem and asked the student to write it on the blackboard and also write the solution. Then he called up a different student and posed a different problem. To me, all the questions seemed rather easy. Some of the students, however, had difficulties. If a student could not do a problem, the professor called out the name of another student and asked him to do it. Some students were asked only one question and, when they answered correctly, were allowed to leave. Others were asked two or more questions, especially if one of the answers was incorrect.

The Spandorfs were called up before me. Both had problems, and both made mistakes. They spent quite a while at the blackboard. At the end, he had to call up a third student because both Spandorfs answered the problem incorrectly. Finally, there were only three or four students left in the class, and I was called. I was given only one problem. As soon as I wrote the answer, he told me I could leave. My answer was correct.

Of course, when I came into the corridor, my mother was wringing her hands with worry. She was sure I must have had trouble since most of the other students were already out. I swiftly assured her that everything was fine and they simply didn't go in alphabetical order this time. She smiled with relief.

Salo came down the hallway from talking to Mrs. Spandorf and saw my mother smiling and squeezing her arm around my shoulders.

"Ah, I can see you did well, right?" he said.

"Yes."

Richard came again to visit and this time brought some friends with him. Again, he quizzed me on my answers and assured me I did well. These visits may not have seemed like much to Richard, but the kindness of it stays with me all my life.

When I discreetly told him about the Spandorfs' poor performance, I added that they probably have enough of influence and don't need to worry about failing.

"In this school," said Richard, "no Jew has any influence."

Until that moment, I had focused all my energy on doing well on the examinations. Now there was only one more trial to go—one more examination. In the back of my mind, I worried I could be turned down because I am a Jew, regardless of how well I might do on the exams. But I couldn't afford to dwell on it.

The bell rang, announcing the final round, and I grimly headed to the classroom, to confront my nemesis, the Polish verbal test. My mother hugged me and nervously whispered in my ear, "*Es soll zein mit mazel.*" Then she said, "Enter the room with your right foot first."

My mother was not generally superstitious, but she didn't want to take any chances. I'm sure, all those hours I was being tested, she was quietly reciting every prayer she thought could help. To accommodate her and superstitious fate, I did a little hop step so I would enter the room with my right foot first.

Once again, we were addressed by three professors. One sat at a desk with our written Polish tests. These he went through one at a time and divided them into two piles: one large and one small. There was total silence in the classroom.

The professor picked up the paper from the top of the large pile and called out the name of the student. This student was asked to write two or three words on the blackboard. I noticed that one of them was misspelled.

The professor then picked up a paper from the other smaller pile and called for another student to step to the board.

"Do you think these words are spelled correctly?" asked the professor.

"No," the boy replied.

"Which one? Write the correct spelling next to it." The boy corrected the misspelled word. The professor then asked the first student to write some more words on the blackboard, which he wrote correctly. After asking him a few questions about Polish history, which he also answered correctly, he told him he could leave the class. The professor made some notes on the first student's examination and put it aside.

Then he examined the paper of the boy who had corrected the misspelled word. The professors asked him some historical dates. He answered correctly and was told he could leave the class.

This pattern repeated itself, and I soon realized the smaller pile must have been the written tests that were good. Students from that pile were usually asked one or two questions. If answered correctly, they were released. So, I nervously wondered: which pile was my test in?

When my name was called, I didn't notice from which pile the professor picked up my paper. My heart was pounding as I walked to the board. Then I realized a student was already at the board and I would be asked to make a correction. So my paper must have come from the good pile.

The student had written the name of the Polish king on the board in answer to his question. I knew it was the wrong answer.

When I reached the blackboard, the professor asked, "You heard the question?"

"Yes," I replied calmly.

"Is this correct?"

"No," I said in a more subdued tone.

"What is the name of the king?"

"Kazimierz Wielki."

While I answered, the professor looked over what must have been my paper. Every second seemed to me like an hour. Maybe my answer was wrong. Could it be? In my ears, I heard my heartbeat race.

The professor lifted up his head and smiled. "You can go," he said.

What a relief! It was as if a 100-pound bag that was on top of my head just fell off. It's amazing how a mood can change so abruptly. I almost ran out of that classroom.

Once again, my mother's face cleared when she saw mine. "I can see everything went well. Right?"

"Right," I said, as if I had just regained my voice.

It was great to walk out of the building between my mother and Salo. I told them in detail what happened in the classroom as we walked home.

One would assume I would stop worrying now that I had evidence that I had done well in Polish, my weak point. But this assumption is not correct. I guess I'm just a worrier by nature. What began as a feeling of confidence slowly changed into a creeping uncertainty. But I wanted to conceal that uncertainty from my mother. A realization came to me that seemed amazing; when I saw my mother in worry and pain, I too felt some of her pain. I guessed that is what is called love. Comparing this with the agonies I had experienced over Mala, it seemed incomprehensible to me that love, which is supposed to be good, was so closely united with pain.

When we got home, all three of us told my father it went well.

"He did very well," my mother told him. "The Spandorf boys, though, not so good."

"Don't worry about the Spandorfs," my father said. "They have money. They probably have all the teachers in their pocket."

It was not that we were poor. Some of my school friends and some boys from our street occasionally used to say, "You don't have to worry. You father is rich." But at home, listening to conversations between my parents, it would seem that they were constantly struggling to keep the business going and always seemed to be short of money. It was confusing to me.

"Did you see Professor Sprecher?" asked my father.

"Yes," my mother said. "But only for a brief moment as he was going into the director's office. He said we should not worry, everything will be fine. There were a lot of people standing there, so we couldn't talk much."

"I guess now all that is left is to wait until tomorrow and hope for the best," said my father. His voice was calm, but it was easy to see he was also anxious to see me pass the exam and get accepted to the school.

We sat down to dinner. It didn't escape my mother's notice that I could not eat. Her anxiety rose quickly.

"What are you worrying about?" she bawled. "You told me you did well. So why do you worry? Come on, eat. It is good for you."

But I just fiddled with my food. My father leaned toward me. Almost whispering, he said, "*Dummkopf* (Stupid)! What are you worrying about? You told everybody you did well. But, even if not, the world will not stop turning. One never knows, but maybe this could turn out even better for you. That is why you should not worry." He chewed some food and then added, "Tomorrow, we shall see."

I knew what he said was right and reasonable. But reason alone was not enough to turn off the worrying machine. All I could think about was telling Richard and my friends that I failed. And losing any hope of ever speaking to Mala.

The Barracks

As I wrote about my exams in my cheap notebook in the Sojma camp in Siberia, all the tension and stress of the experience returned to me. I forgot where I was. It was even a surprise to look up and find myself in the barracks. My pencil was getting smaller. I hoped it would last long enough for me to write about the day after the examinations—the day we got the results.

14

Results

The morning after my exams, I returned to the school with my father, mother, and Lisa. We would learn who had passed and who would be accepted into the *gymnasium*. It was about 9:30 in the morning. I had eaten no breakfast. As we walked, we did not converse, as if going to a funeral. I wished again I could turn back the clock so that I would do better in Polish.

Just a few minutes ahead of us was a moment that I knew would mark my life forever, one way or the other. Walking toward it, I felt I knew a little of what a condemned man feels as he walks to the gallows.

In the busy hallway, we found Professor Sprecher. My father spoke to him. He explained he was not involved in the grading of exams for my group, so he did not know what the decision was. However, he assured my father that I had done well.

As we made our way to the auditorium, my father told my mother, "He doesn't know any more than we do. All we can do now is hope for the best."

The students and their families assembled in the auditorium. On the stage, behind the podium, was a long row of chairs for faculty members. I sat between my parents. Professor Sprecher came and sat with us, next to Lisa. The auditorium was full. A nervous hubbub of sound was in the room until a line of professors came out on stage and took their seats. The silence was complete when the school director walked to the podium. My heart thumped against my rib cage. The director cleared his throat.

"In a moment, I will read the names of the students who took the exam. I will say if the student passed or did not pass. However, I must explain we have 560 applicants and only space for 126 new students. Because of this limit, only those students with the best results have been accepted. Those students who passed the exam but were not accepted will be able to apply and take an exam again next year. They will be given priority in acceptance. Those who did not pass the exam can also reapply next year, but they will not be given priority."

Now I felt a black cloud of doom over me. Passing was not enough. I had to be among the best. It seemed a lost cause. Why had I even put my family and myself through the agony?

He began to read names. They were not in alphabetical order, so I strained my ears and kept my eyes on the director's lips for each name. The first fifteen names were followed by "*nie zdal*" (did not pass). Finally there was the name of a student followed by "*zdal*" (passed). Then there were another eight or ten names with *nie zdal*. Then a name followed by "*odwierzony*" (not accepted). Then another long stretch of *nie zdal*.

He called a name. A boy sitting near me drew in his breath sharply and sat bolt upright.

"*Nie zdal.*"

The boy collapsed back against his chair and began sobbing. When I saw that, I almost lost my nerve and started sobbing myself. His red-faced mother tried to comfort him. They were sitting in the middle of an aisle, like us, and could not get up to leave. They had to sit through the whole ordeal. My whole body started aching.

"*Nie zdal…nie zdal…nie zdal.*" The sledgehammer rhythm of the director's voice pounded the crowd lower and lower. The rare *zdal* or *odwierzony* only made the steady *nie zdal* beat seem more oppressive. Of the seven Jewish applicants, the first three were *nie zdal, nie zdal,* and *nie zdal.*

My mother's face was red and taut with worry. My father and Lisa managed to show no emotion, but they were listening intently. Professor Sprecher looked completely calm.

"Gustaf Spandorf," the director read. "*Nie zdal.*" I heard a gasp from the crowd. "Otto Spandorf, *nie zdal.*"

My father turned away from me toward Lisa. "That's it," he told her. "If the Spandorfs were turned down, you cannot expect an Eichel to be accepted."

"Who knows?" Lisa said. "Not much hope, I guess."

The words were no sooner out of her mouth when we heard, "Simon Eichel…"

My heart stopped. Even though I was looking at the director at the podium as he announced my name, I could not believe my ears. A wave of heat engulfed me as if I had fallen into the furnace at the King's Steelworks. At the same time, it felt as if I was flying somewhere in the clouds and my only contact with the world was my ears. And then, after what seemed like ages, I heard "*zdal.*" I passed!

It was as if someone hit my head with a hammer and knocked out all the tension, fear, and worry. I crashed back to earth, but it felt like heaven. My ears were ringing with, "Simon Eichel, *zdal*. Simon Eichel, *zdal*. Simon Eichel, *zdal*."

My mother leaped from her seat and embraced me, and kissed me on my forehead again and again, so hard that it began to hurt. She dropped back to her seat, her face bursting with joy. My father was smiling too, but with a quizzical look on his face, as if he was trying to contemplate: "The Spandorfs, no. But my son, yes!" But what he actually said aloud—to no one in particular—was, "Are you sure he said *zdal*?"

Lisa was smiling broadly. She reached out to shake hands with Professor Sprecher.

"I told you he would pass," he said.

"Are you sure he said *zdal*?" repeated my father.

The rest of the names passed by in a drone as I let the news wash over me. I could tell Richard! Mala would hear about it! I would not have to become a tailor!

As soon as the director finished, most people got up to leave. My father announced he was going to ask the director to verify that I passed. He took me by the hand and we walked to the podium. Some people were talking to the director, who seemed annoyed and anxious to get away. We waited until they finished.

He then asked the director, "Can you please check if my son passed? Simon Eichel?"

"I called out every name," said the director, clearly irritated. "Didn't you hear me?" My father only looked at him expectantly. "What group was he in?" the director demanded. My father had no idea.

"Third, sir," I said.

The director flipped through some pages. "What is the name?"

"Simon Eichel," said my father.

The director scanned the page for a long moment and then stopped. He lifted his head and looked directly at my father. "*Zdal*."

"Did you say *zdal*?" my father asked, still not believing.

"Yes, man!" shouted the director. "*Zdal! Zdal!*"

"Thank you," said my father apologetically.

I led him away before he could ask the director to repeat it yet again. We went to my mother and Lisa.

"He passed," said my father in a tone of voice suitable for a miracle.

"I know it," said my mother.

On the street, we met Richard and some of his friends. When my mother saw Richard, she squeezed me and shouted, "He passed!"

I tried to act cool when Richard came forward to shake my hand, but I could not contain the huge grin that blossomed on my face.

"Well done!" said Richard.

"Thank you."

As we walked home, I felt I knew a little of what a man feels walking away from the gallows after a miraculous reprieve. The sun was shining and everything my eye fell upon was glorious and new.

"You know," my mother said to my father, "you'll have to make him a uniform."

"Yes."

"No, he'll need two."

"Two?"

"One for every day, and one for weekends and holidays."

"I don't know how I will make one uniform, and already you are talking about two." My father rolled his eyes.

My mother grabbed me again and kissed me and whispered "Don't worry. You'll be well-dressed for school."

My head was overflowing with joy and pride. I felt like jumping and screaming from happiness, right there in the street. However, now that I was a *gymnasiast*, a member of the educated class, I could no longer act childish. So I restrained myself. But in my mind, I saw myself walking around in the new uniform with Richard and his friends. I saw myself walking with Mala. I walked like Mala, as if I had a crown on my head, proud and composed.

But that composure only lasted until we got to the apartment. As soon as I got inside, I began jumping up and down like a little kid.

I shouted, "*Zdal, zdal, zdal!*"

Salo, Moniek, and Hannele looked at me in disbelief.

"He passed?" Salo asked.

"Not only did he pass," my father trumpeted, "but he was the only Jew who passed!" Until he said that, I had not realized it. My father looked at me apologetically and said, "I know we all were 100 percent sure you would not pass."

"Not me!" screamed my mother, thrusting her finger upward in a triumphant gesture. "Not me!"

We sat down for the dinner that Hannele had made. I was treated as if this was my birthday. Now, my appetite was ravenous, and everything tasted good. After dinner, my mother took me aside where no one could see. She quietly pushed a whole zloty into my hand.

She didn't say anything, but her eyes were shining as if to say "This is for you. You deserve it."

A zloty was a lot of money for me; more than I had ever gotten from anyone. At Hanukah, we used to get five groszen. The biggest gift ever was thirty or forty groszen to go to a movie.

A few minutes later my father called me over and in front of the family and grandly bestowed on me fifty groszen, half of what my mother gave. He said I could use it to go to the movies. I thanked him. Neither I nor my mother told him about her gift.

Throughout the afternoon, neighbors dropped by to congratulate me. Everyone in our house was happy, except maybe Moniek, who was jealous of all the attention I was getting.

Koltunov's Pants

The hardship of life at Sojma then took a significant turn for the better. One day, Commandant Koltunov came to inspect the camp. As he was passing my father, he accidentally tore his pants on a sharp twig. He cursed robustly in Russian, looking at the tear. My father stepped forward and told the commandant he was a custom tailor. He said he could fix the tear so that no one could ever tell it was there. The commandant nodded and told my father to come to his office after work.

That evening, after fixing the tear, my father told how happy the commandant was with the work and how friendly and generous he was. My father fixed some other garments for him and was paid more than he could earn working in the woods. But most importantly, the commandant had agreed to my father's request to get a sewing machine.

A few weeks later, the commandant returned with a hand sewing machine that we considered an antique. He also brought along some other garments, including uniforms from officers in other settlements. Some came from as far away as Khanty-Mansiysk, the headquarters of the NKVD, which was more than 100 kilometers from Sojma.

With the approval of the commandant, my father arranged for some workspace in the little log cabin between the barracks and the *stolovaja* that served as the infirmary. There was a small room in the back that my father took.

With that old machine, my father was in business again. He no longer had to work in the woods. Frequently officers came from other distant places and brought work for him. They paid handsomely from our point of view, yet they viewed it as a tremendous bargain, and even a convenience.

Soon, my father had Salo working for him. Later, there was so much work he brought in two more tailors from our camp. The money was good, but the most important thing was that they no longer had to endure the hardship of working outdoors and in the woods. Though Hassenberg used to tease my father that all he did in the woods was supervise us. Salo, however, never got used to that work and was always complaining of feeling sick. That was a great relief for all of us.

The Bude

After the summer of 1937, Moniek and I returned home from vacation a week before school started. We had stayed with Lisa in Rabka Zdroj in the mountains. It took my father three days to make my *gymnasium* uniform. It was the first time in my life that I wore long pants. I spent the last days with Richard and his friends, showing off my new uniform. They assured me it would not be too long before I would be happy whenever I could get out of the uniform and walk around in casual clothes. After all, they already had two years of experience.

They warned me about the difficulties in learning Latin, a mandatory and most hated subject. They talked so much about it that I really got scared. However, I was so happy they had something to talk about with me and that they finally regarded me as a peer. We walked around in the park together, and they also took me along to the Akiba, the Zionist organization that they all belonged to.

I was normally a late riser, and my mother had to urge me to be ready for school. But the morning of my first day at The Bude, I woke without help, two hours before school. After a hasty breakfast, I dressed in my new uniform, took a notepad and a new pen and pencil set, and left for the *gymnasium*. I got to school a half hour early. A list of students by classroom was posted on the bulletin board in the entrance hallway. I noticed I was the only Jew in my class.

I went up to my third-floor classroom. It was empty and quiet, like a soccer field before the teams arrive. A sheet of school regulations was posted on the bulletin board:

- Overcoats and caps must be placed in the wardrobe cabinets in the hallway. Each class was assigned their own hangers and shelf space.

- Each student must be clean and dressed in the complete school uniform.

- Students must carry school identification cards at all times.

- Students must behave properly while on school grounds and outside the school.

There were many more regulations, covering every activity in the school. Students began filtering into the room in groups of two or three. I recognized some of them from the entry examination.

Because there were no seating assignments, you could choose where you wanted to sit. There were three rows of double desk and chair sets. At first, I was not sure if I should take a seat in the front or the back. Most of the students sat together in groups. They probably came from the same school. Some groups took the front seats, others the back. The classroom was filling up quickly. I noticed one empty desk in the middle row I quickly sat down and put my notebook on the top of the desk. The seat next to me was empty. Just as the bell rang, a student hurried in and sat next to me. He started conversing with the student sitting in front of us.

Then the professor entered the classroom. He introduced himself as Professor Krawiecki and explained he would teach two subjects: Polish history and German language. He announced some class rules and suggested we read the school rules posted on the wall in the hallway. He emphasized that the behavior of the students in the school as well as outside the school was very important. He then pointed to a bulletin board on the wall in the classroom and explained any important announcements would be posted there. It was the duty of every student to check the board daily and make sure to read all new bulletins. He explained the class must be kept clean and ready at all times. Therefore, every week two students would be assigned the following duties:

- Pick up the classroom keys in the superintendent's office, and open the classroom fifteen minutes prior to the start of classes (7:45 AM).

- Wipe the blackboard clean in the morning and during recess. See to it there is chalk and a washcloth ready at the board.

- Replenish the ink in the ink glass on each desk, including his, as needed.

- Lock the classroom, and return the keys to the superintendent's office.

He explained, every Friday morning, the names of four students would be posted. The first two would be responsible for that week's duties. The other two were only substitutes in case one or both students on duty were absent.

He then informed us that there were two books kept in the director's office. In the black book, every infraction of a rule was listed. Any student who was so distinguished three times would be automatically expelled from school. In the gold book, students who ended a year with excellent marks in every subject would be listed.

Then he picked up a list and began to read the roll call. Soon he called out, "Eichel?"

I stood up and said, "Here."

"Eichel," he asked, "what is your first name?"

"Simon."

"Why do I have Siegfried here?"

I explained that at home I was called Siegfried and my public school certificates carried that name.

"What is the name on your birth certificate?" he asked.

"Simon," I answered.

"Well," he asked, "why use a name that sounds German when you have such a good, Polish name? I am crossing out Siegfried. As a Polish citizen, you should be proud of your Polish name, Simon."

"Yes, sir." I said.

I have to admit I was getting uncomfortably warm; almost sweating. I was very much relieved when he finally told me to sit down and proceeded to call out other names. When he finished, he explained that, for the first few days, it would be difficult for him to remember all our names. So, whenever a student in the class was called upon, he should announce his full name first.

He barely finished talking when the bell rang, ending the homeroom period. Professor Krawiecki dismissed the class and we walked down to the schoolyard for a recess period. At first, I felt lonely in the schoolyard. Most of the students were in groups, and I didn't know anyone. After a while, I met the two Jewish students from the upper classes and I walked with them.

When recess ended, we went back to our third-floor classroom. During the next hour, Professor Krawiecki gave us the weekly schedule for the first half of the school year. I was relieved to know that Latin was not in my curriculum.

The professor asked for all Protestant students to raise their hands. Two did. Then he asked all Jewish students to raise their hands. I was the only one. I felt very uneasy, to say the least. I sensed that to advertise that I was Jewish certainly was not the best thing for me. I expected some snickering, but, to my surprise, the class was quiet.

The professor then announced that, for religious hour, there would be separate classes for Protestant and Jewish students. The rabbi would conduct the Jewish hour twice a week in a different classroom. Religious hour for the Catholics would take place in our classroom.

And so began my first school year in The Bude. In the next few days we got acquainted with the other professors, all of whom seemed to be nice. The first half year was not too hard for me since we basically repeated things we learned in public school. To my surprise, I found the math hour pretty boring. Some students in our class had problems, and, before long, I was regarded as the best in math. However, Polish language remained a tough subject for me. At my mother's urging, everyone at home continued to speak to me only in Polish. Salo occasionally made me spell some difficult words, or he corrected my sentences. I was pleasantly surprised when at the end of the half year I received a "good" mark for Polish.

I was among the best students in history, biology, and physics. I was good in geography too but I didn't like the professor. He always had an oily smile on his face and thought he had a clever sense of humor.

I was not that good in German grammar, even though I spoke well. But I was also near the top of the class in this subject because many could not speak German at all. In gymnastics, I was not the greatest, but I did not belong to the "clumsy" group either.

At the end of the first half year, my report card had only "good" and "very good" marks on all subjects. I have to note that I was very proud of the results and so were my parents, especially my mother.

The fact that I was the only Jew accepted to The Bude earned me a great deal of respect, not only by Richard and his friends but also by Mala and her girl-friends. At first, when they saw me, they stopped and congratulated me. I cannot describe the feeling, except to say it was as close to heaven that one could ever get. Only a person who has been kept outside a group can know how it feels to finally gain admittance. Afterward, when we passed on the street, they would acknowledge my greeting and occasionally even exchange a few words. They knew I was alive. I now belonged to the Akiba and made a lot of friends there. I confess the pride went into my head, and I became somewhat snobbish myself. I no longer played or talked to the boys on the street. I became selective in choosing my friends.

In the second half year, the much-dreaded event arrived: Latin. But to my surprise, I found that it was really not bad. In fact, I was getting pretty good grades on my work and enjoying it. Most of the students in our class hated this subject, but I didn't let that bother me. One of the reasons was the professor. It's curious to me that I don't remember his name because I remember him clearly. He was tall and slender, generally good-looking and well-dressed. He was extremely strict, but always fair. None of the other professors were as strict, and students felt much more at ease in their classes. Sometimes during classes with Dr. Obrzod, the Polish professor, students talked to each other so loudly that you could hardly hear the professor when he spoke. Not so during Latin.

The professor showed no favoritism. You could be the best student, but, if you made a few mistakes, you got a D and a strong reprimand, just as the poor student would get. We students feared his displeasure and were united in our dislike of him. At least that's what we thought. A year later, when he transferred to another school, we all wept when he came to our classroom to bid us good-bye. We wondered why, only a few days ago, we hated him and now found ourselves crying and praising him.

Early in the second half year in math class, I turned in a test to Professor Kozlowski. As usual, I was the first to finish.

He looked at his watch and said, "That took you twenty-one minutes. For you, that is much too long. You can do better."

I was shocked. He made no such comments to any other student. At first, I thought he was being anti-Semitic. But soon, he also gave me encouraging remarks as well. He continued to time my work and tried to challenge me. He must have noticed I was bored.

As the year progressed, I developed a cordial friendship with some of my classmates. I was pleasantly surprised that there were no incidents because of my being Jewish.

The exception to this rule occurred in the latter half of my second year at The Bude in 1939, and it was brought on not by a student, but by a professor.

Professor Marszak, my geography teacher, described a recent trip of his to the city of Lublin. I can still see the self-satisfied smirk on his face as he spoke.

"When I arrived in Lublin," he said with an airy and falsely convivial tone, "there were a number of *droszkas* (horse carriages) lined up in front of the railroad station. I needed a ride to the hotel, so I took the first *droszka* in the lineup. As we were driving, I noticed the driver had a long beard and long sideburns dangling from his face."

With his hands, he comically outlined the facial hair, provoking peals of laughter from some of the students. He went on to describe the driver in the most derogatory terms. He did not say the man was a Jew, but the meaning was clear to everyone. Marszak did not make eye contact with me, but some of my classmates were staring at me and smiling. I had expected anti-Semitic actions—if they came at all—to come from the students and to come during recess or in the hall; never in the class, and never from a professor in such a direct way. I was unprepared and completely humiliated before Marszak lightly delivered the coup de grace.

"I think this will be a good subject for homework," he said, as if the inspired idea had just dawned on him. "Jews in Poland."

I looked down at my desk in shame, my face burning hot.

"I will name two students who will prepare a written report for next week," he said. He swung his arm, pointing his finger to the far side of the class, and thrust it toward a student. "Bartok," he said, naming the son of a prominent anti-Semite. Then he swung his finger back toward my side. He seemed to search randomly, but I was not surprised when he smiled and said, "Eichel."

The gauntlet was thrown down. I had to pick it up by writing a good paper. But I had no idea what to write about. There was no information on this subject in the geography textbook, beyond a few lines on population statistics. When I got home, I asked Salo about it. He suggested I talk to the rabbi of our synagogue, who was also the one who provided religious instruction at the *gymnasium*.

The rabbi gave me a list of books and suggested I use only factual quotes and statistics, and be prepared to identify the source of my information. I did a lot of reading that week and had many sleepless nights.

The day before the assignment was due, Bartok announced that he had his report ready. Professor Marszak, who did not seem at all surprised by this announcement, asked Bartok to read it to the class. I immediately felt defensive. I could have had mine done that day, too.

Bartok's voice had a confident intonation as he read from his paper. He described Jews in the most demeaning way and stated that Jews were a burden to Poland, not a help, and that they came to the country uninvited.

At that, I raised my hand and said, "That statement is historically incorrect." I knew it was King Kazimirez who invited German Jews to come to Poland to help boost the Polish trade about 500 years ago. The king issued a decree that established ghettos where those Jews could live safely and stated they were not allowed to own land.

But Marszak didn't let me continue. "At the end of the presentation," he said, "there will be a class discussion. In the meantime, just take notes."

But when Bartok was finished, the professor said, "That was a truly excellent presentation. There really is no need for discussion."

I felt numb. After class was dismissed, a group of students approached me in the hall. One of them was Hanke, the son of the president of the city council. They all confirmed that Bartok made some mistaken assertions. They all encouraged me to point them out when I presented my report the following day.

When that day came, and I began to read, students fired questions at me left and right. I couldn't finish a paragraph. The professor remained silent. I answered each of them with direct quotes from one of my books.

After a number of such interruptions, Hanke stood up.

"Look," he said, "let's pick just two students to ask questions. I'll help Eichel in answering them. That way, we can have a fair discussion."

I was surprised at this and happily nodded my agreement. It was not only because I felt outnumbered, but it was also because Hanke was one of the brightest students in the class.

"Sit down, Hanke," said the professor. "Eichel does not need a lawyer. Anyway, I am his best advocate, and I want everyone in class to participate."

So I continued reading and wading through the questions. Then I concluded with some statistics recently published by the government. "Jews constitute about ten percent of the population in Poland. About twenty percent of Jews are considered to be illiterate. In comparison, almost fifty percent of the entire Polish population is considered illiterate. Also, a much greater percentage of Jews are in professions requiring higher education. This indicates that most Jews in Poland are educated and intelligent people."

At this point, Professor Marszak jumped up from his chair.

"Does anyone want to comment on this last statement?" he asked. No one did. He turned to me and archly said, "I do not dispute the statistics, but the fact that one is educated does not mean one is also intelligent. As a matter of fact, I know quite a few educated people who behave like pigs and are certainly not intelligent."

He sat down abruptly and pulled out his grading notebook with great deliberation. "This presentation deserves a D," he said.

I was stunned, then doubly stunned again as I heard sounds of angry disapproval from the class.

"No!" some said.

Hanke's voice loudly said "That is not fair."

To my continued amazement, the professor relented a little. "Well, I guess a C is about right."

I sighed with great relief.

When the class was dismissed, a number of students came over to apologetically explain that they were asking so many questions not because I was wrong, but only to gain some favorable points with the professor. Hanke openly sneered at them.

My relief at having successfully negotiated the perils of Professor Marszak soon vanished.

A few days later, I went to the movies with my friend Salek Friedman, one of Richard's classmates. We decided to stay in the theater and watch the same picture again. It ended about ten minutes after eight in the evening, which was the curfew hour for all students from our *gymnasium*. As we left the theater, we almost bumped directly into none other than Professor Marszak. There was no doubt in my mind that he recognized me. I was certain to wind up in the black book.

The next day at school, I expected to be called in to the director's office. I went straight to the bulletin board, but, to my surprise, no notice was posted there. I was relieved, but I was also suspicious and sick with worry about what would happen later that day in geography class.

When that class arrived and Professor Marszak strolled into the room, he breezily said, "Nowadays, it isn't even safe for a professor to walk on the street after eight in the evening and not be almost knocked over by a student." But he never mentioned my name, and I was not called into the director's office.

I would not have predicted, at the year end, that I would get a "good" in geography, but that's what Professor Marszak gave me. All my other grades were "good" and "excellent," and I was proud. So was my father, but my mother was just bursting. To practically everyone she spoke to, she found an excuse to brag about me.

It was almost the only joy she had in the summer of 1939.

15

Cierniakov's Bet

Writing about my school experiences gave me some relief from the Siberian winter and the hard life at Sojma. After the arrival of the sewing machine, we prospered a little. It was my father's way to seem almost a little superstitious when things were going well, as if he feared that enjoyment of good times would bring them crashing down. He would intone his old phrase, "God does not give with both hands. If he gives you something with one, he takes something away with the other."

One night, I was walking outside. It was dark, and I repeatedly tripped over rocks and other small obstacles in my path. The next evening, the same thing happened again. I could barely see the people walking with me and sometimes bumped into them.

They scolded me. "Watch where you are going." When I tripped again, they said, "What? Are you blind? Didn't you see that big stone?"

But I didn't see it. I began to realize that my night vision had grown poor. I kept on tripping, and it's lucky I didn't fall down and break my neck.

As time went on I noticed that, during the day, the glare of sunlight off the snow was blinding me. It began to sink in that something was very wrong with my eyes. We had a doctor among our people and he looked at me and explained that I suffered from scurvy, a lack of vitamin A found in fresh vegetables and fruits. I had not eaten such foods since leaving Chorzow. There was little of it to be had in Lvov. At Sojma, it was not available at any price.

Other people were getting sick as well. Some lost most of their teeth and then their legs would swell so badly that they could hardly walk. I was the only one who was going blind. It was frightening to imagine being able to only see a glare of white during the day and only black darkness at night. It was impossible to imagine being denied the ability to read.

At this time, my father was "invited" by a *nachalnik* (high-ranking government official) to come to his home and do some tailoring. His home was in

Khanty-Mansiysk, the headquarters of the Regional Government Offices more than 100 kilometers away. The only means of transportation in the wintertime was by open horse-drawn sled. We didn't think my father could make such a trip through the wilderness with temperatures of forty below in constant snowstorms. He was fifty-nine years old. On the other hand, refusing would be disastrous. You could not simply say "No, thank you" to a *nachalnik*.

My father told Commandant Koltunov he was not feeling well and would send Salo instead. Anyway, he said Salo was now running the tailoring operations like he did at home in Chorzow. Most of the visiting officers also knew Salo, and he was very friendly with both the Commandant Koltunov and his deputy, Cierniakov.

It was agreed, and Salo was the first to leave the camp and see Khanty-Mansiysk. Cierniakov drove him there in the sled. He stayed for two or three days, worked and slept in the *nachalnik's* home and ate with his family.

When he came back, he described, in delicious detail, all the foods he ate. Josel and I smacked our lips fantasizing. But, more important than stories, Salo brought back a jar of fish oil. He had told them about my plight, and they said this would be good for me. I took two tablespoons, three times a day. It tasted awful, like the castor oil we used at home for constipation.

But it worked like a miracle. The very first evening, I could already see better. After a week, I was back to normal. The other good thing that came from it was that I was given preferential treatment of foods from then on, especially stuff Salo or my father used to get from their clients.

Salo was popular with the *nachalniks*, and he began making more trips to Khanty-Mansiysk. Even though things were getting slightly better for all of us, Josel and I continued to be hungry most of the day. But we had learned to handle the weather and to work better.

We also learned to cheat a little bit. We quietly learned a technique from one of the other work groups whose productivity seemed much higher than the rest. When we cut a stack of logs, an inspector would examine it, credit it to our group, and put markings on the end of the stack to indicate it had been counted. Sometimes, once a stack had been counted, we simply moved it to another place, taking care to hide the inspection marks. This way, we were credited for the same stack twice. There were some other variations on this theme, and they always worked. The error was never discovered until we completed loading the logs on the rafts. Then, when the totals always seemed short, the Russian inspector would be blamed for doing a careless job. He would be replaced, and the game would begin again. No one was ever caught.

The winter was cold, long, and dark. It was dark when we went to work in the morning. Eight hours later, it was dark again when we came back to the camp. We were very glad when the winter began to pass and the days got longer and warmer. The ice on the river began melting and the rafts with the logs drifted north. Soon, a tugboat showed up and pulled a long caravan of rafts up the river. We were told it was going up to the tundra, where nothing grows, all the way to the town of Salehard near the Arctic Circle.

If working in the woods in winter was bad, we soon found out that working in the spring was not much better. With swamps all around, we were constantly besieged by maddening swarms of mosquitoes. And these were not the weak variety that annoys us in the cities during a European summer. They were aggressive, vigorous beasts who bit hard. No matter how warm it was, we had to wear long-sleeved shirts that were buttoned up as much as possible and long pants. And, just like in the wintertime, your face was always exposed. Waving them off with one arm was an eternal task that grew to seem silly until the moment you stopped. Then they were on you again. I preferred the cold, any day.

What annoyed us almost as much was the fact that the Russians working in the woods seemed to be less troubled by the mosquitoes than we were. It was as if the insects had something personal against us. The Russians almost never waved off bugs with their hands. Josel wisecracked, while fanning the hordes away from his face, that even the mosquitoes had a nonaggression pact with the Russians.

I don't know how, but eventually we learned to live with it and treat it like a simple nuisance more than a hindrance to work. It was either that or go stark raving mad.

That spring, Commandant Koltunov called for volunteers to build some additional houses. They would be two-room buildings assigned to families or selected groups of individuals. They would be set about 100 meters behind the barracks. This would ease some of the overcrowding in our barracks. A Russian would supervise each volunteer crew, and those who volunteered would be given priority for the new housing.

On the surface, this project appealed to me. It would be a relief to have some different kind of work for a change and, of course, it would be much better to live in a house than the barracks.

The bad thing was that it meant they were planning for us to stay there a long time. We were not prepared to accept that. Survival was easier if we hoped the war would end soon and we could go back home. We talked about this.

The winter already had exacted some casualties. Many people had frozen toes. Some were sick, and one person had died. It was hard to keep desperation away.

The house project just made the desperation more acute. Hope is what kept us alive.

When one of us complained of not feeling so well, my father frequently said, "You have got to fight this. Stay strong! So when the time comes—and it will come soon—we can go back."

Though it dealt a blow to our hopes, Josel and I volunteered.

"Who knows?" we thought. "Maybe the war will end before we even finish building."

Anyway, we wanted a better living arrangement for my father. Four groups were formed of about six to eight people, mostly young men. The supervisor of our group was a withdrawn, young man in his late twenties named Kiriak. He was patient and never lost his cool, unlike some of the others. We frequently heard them screaming the standard Russian obscenities.

Kiriak showed us how to lay the foundation, trim the bark off the trees, and slightly flatten the space on the logs so they fit properly on top of each other with minimum space in between. He showed us how to chop out a deep enough notch at the end of the log so that they lock and create a ninety-degree-angle corner. Most of it was done by using our axes only and, occasionally, the saw. Except for a level, we used no other tool.

Kiriak used his ax with ease and accuracy, as if it was part of his body. When he chopped a notch, it fit perfectly the first time. Plus, he was fast. We were getting better at it, but Kiriak was an artist.

Kiriak instructed Josel to cut a stack of boards to fit the floor. The word for floor in Russian is *pol*, which, in Polish, sounds like the word for half. So, Josel measured the boards and cut them in half. He looked bewildered as Kiriak lost his cool for the first time, swearing red-faced and waving his arms in frustration. When he saw the error of his ways, Josel got some more boards and made the floor properly.

We cut boards from selected straight logs using a simple operation. The tree was placed on top of two wooden poles crossed like an "X" at each end. The midpoint of the X was about six feet high. One man would stay on the top of the log and another immediately below him. They would use a six-foot-long two-handed saw. Starting at one end of the log, they cut about two-inch thick boards the length of the log by pulling the saw up and down as they went.

As always with the two-handed saw, timing was everything. One young man from the Polish city of Lodz, was named Jankel. When he cut boards, he sang a rhythmic song to help his timing: *Ich bin ein jing fun Lodzr kant/and wert fabrent mit enker land.* It was a defiant rhyme meaning, "I am a young man from Lodz, and may you burn with your land."

One day, Commandant Koltunov visited while we were cutting boards. He nodded with the rhythm of the singing and then turned to Josel.

"This song," he said. "What does it mean?" Some of us started to smile and turn our faces away. Josel, of course, didn't hesitate.

"He comes from the city of Lodz, but he loves this beautiful land."

Koltunov eyed Josel for a moment. Then he nodded his approval and went on to inspect the construction. Later, when he and I were alone, I said, "Josel, my God. That was really good."

"Schmoy-boy."

About two months later the house was finished. It had two rooms with an iron stove in the middle. There were no doors between the rooms. We made all the furniture ourselves, including the beds and a six-foot-long table with benches on each side. We chose Hassenberg, Franzel, and Kagan to stay in our house with my father, Salo, Josel, and me.

Kagan was a banker from Warsaw. Although we respected his intelligence, he was helpless in our present circumstance. We felt sorry for him.

Franzel was a young man from Vienna who was one of three who tried escaping a few weeks after our arrival in Sojma. Nobody even knew they were missing. The first two men came back after a couple of days wandering through the swamps. They were lucky to find the way back. When they returned, they told us Franzel was still out there.

The following day, poor Franzel walked back into the camp. He looked like he had just returned from hell. Mosquito bites covered his hands and face. He was put into the jail, a dried-up outhouse with a bench, for three days. Everybody admired Franzel's courage, but his attempt also made everybody realize what the commandant had said to us was true. Escape was out of the question.

The new homes altered the lifestyle in Sojma. Since we were not as much on top of each other all the time, there was a little more privacy, better sleeping conditions, and a better social life. Social groups and even couples began to form.

In the house next to ours lived a group of young men and women. They were the first group that came up with the idea of restacking the woodpiles. One of the women, Anna, was pretty and in her midtwenties. She paired up with Marcus Immergluck, a tall, good-looking man a few years older than she was. Other couples like that were in the other houses. Some of those men and women who paired up may not have been single in their prewar marital status.

Our house wasn't the only one that was occupied predominantly by a single family. There were also the Siegal and Hochman families. The elder Siegal had a big, white beard like a rabbi, and he was a respected elder in the camp. In their house lived a man named Brenner who later married Siegal's daughter.

There was definitely a livelier atmosphere on our block of houses than there was in the barracks. I could even say it was jovial.

Some of the women in the houses had started to cook. The main dish was mushrooms they gathered in the woods. One day, my father came home and told us he watched Mrs. Siegal prepare and cook the mushrooms. He said there was no reason why we couldn't do the same.

We followed the women to the woods and learned which mushrooms were edible. Between Salo, Josel, Franzel, Hassenberg, me, and my father (supervising), we soon had a big bag of mushrooms. Our family whistle helped keep us from getting lost in the woods, which was otherwise very easy to do.

In the store, we bought a big *chugun*, a cast-iron cooking pot shaped like a casserole with a narrow base. It was the biggest pot I had ever seen. It probably held ten gallons of water and weighed a ton. But that was not a problem for Josel or me. We wanted volume.

When we cleaned the mushrooms, we cut out some of the worms and bad spots before they went into the pot. Josel, Franzel, and I were very careful not to cut too much out of the mushrooms we cleaned. But Salo was just the opposite. He frequently kept on pulling out of the pot the mushrooms we already had cleaned, admonishing us to cut out more. We admonished him right back to cut out less. My father, as usual, was calm and kept these arguments under control. It was good to eat our own food. By the time we finished, you did not have to wash the pot; it was practically licked clean by Josel and me. But we still were hungry all day. Mushrooms don't satisfy hunger.

We also experimented with making jam, as our neighbor Eva did. Hers tasted delicious. She showed us which berries to pick and we brought them home and boiled them in the *chugun*. We had to constantly scoop off the foam from the top and discard it. But when we finally finished cooking and tasted it, it was bitter like hell. That was one meal that even Josel and I did not eat. We ran to Eva, and she admitted her secret. She had some sugar left over from back home that she had used in her jam.

One night after we had bedded down, I overheard Salo talking to my father. Salo had delivered some work to Koltunov, and the commandant grilled him for an hour, asking him if he heard or knew of anybody who is anti-communist or anti-Russian or said anything against the government. Salo said he did not know anything, and they made him sign a paper that he would not tell anyone about being there and threatened him if he did.

My father told him to make sure he did not say anything, even to Josel or me, explaining, "They may accidentally say something, and you can't take that chance."

A few months later, Josel had the same experience himself. This time, my father made sure Salo and I knew about it. He feared I might be the next to be called in, and he warned me to make sure to not say anything. Josel even said they gave him a printed statement to sign. He made sure to sign immediately below the statement so that nothing could be written in between.

In 1941, Germany invaded Russia. So much for German nonaggression. At first there were no major changes at Sojma, but gradually the items we had in our store became more expensive and scarcer. But we didn't mind this because we knew it must shorten the war, just like in World War I. There were now too many nations against Germany including mighty Russia.

Now that America was a Russian ally, we were allowed to write letters to my father's brothers, Benny and Philip, in New York City. My father knew that the letter would be censored by the NKVD so he was careful. He wrote that we were in Sojma, about 1,000 miles north from Chelabinsk, Siberia, where Benny and Philip were taken in 1905 before they managed to escape.

Shortly after that, my father found out that Mr. Hochman in the camp had a set of barber tools. He wanted fifty rubles, which we could not afford to pay. They negotiated, and Hochman eventually agreed to sell it for twenty-five rubles and free haircuts for himself for as long as we stayed in Sojma. He knew we had written a letter to America, so he added a stipulation that, if we got some money from America, we would owe him another twenty-five rubles. My father thought he must have been joking. Benny and Phillip were not rich, so he agreed.

"It should only happen," he said.

We doubted they would even receive the letter.

Josel now was able to earn some extra money practicing his trade. We all got our first haircut since we left Lvov, and the residents of entire camp took on a tidier look. It was surprising how much that simple thing lifted morale.

Another thing that lifted morale was Cierniakov's bet.

One of the biggest events of our day was bread distribution time in the evening. The loaves, about twenty inches long and weighing about five pounds, were carefully divided and distributed. We would gather around the table in one of the barracks and tell stories, reminisce, joke around, and maybe sing some Jewish songs. It was the primary time for socializing. During mild weather, we would also hang around the river where we washed ourselves and did laundry. But the bread distribution happened all year. Though we lived in a house now, we still received our bread in our old barracks.

One evening, Deputy Commandant Cierniakov dropped by our barracks during bread distribution. He happened to be standing next to Jankel, the fine singer from Lodz, who told him, "I bet you I could eat an entire loaf right now. All by myself."

Jankel always said this. He was cut from the same cloth as Josel and me; always hungry.

Cierniakov was quick to reply. "I bet you can't."

He left the barracks, returning a few minutes later with a full loaf of bread in his hands. He walked over to Jankel.

"We have a bet," he challenged. "You said you could eat the entire loaf of bread at one time."

"Yes," said Jankel, clearly astonished as he eyed the bread. "I said it, and I can do it, too."

"And I say you can't," replied Cierniakov. "Remember, just the bread and nothing else. Not even a sip of water with it." Cierniakov then held the loaf against Jankel's lean abdomen. "I must warn you," he said seriously. There was complete silence in the barracks. "You could get very sick. This bread is bigger than your stomach."

Jankel took the loaf and went to the table. "Make way, comrades," he said. The mute crowd gathered around him in disbelief. I pressed in close, not believing my eyes.

Jankel began to eat, smiling, biting into the crust of the loaf, holding it in his two hands. He ate almost a quarter of it before his zeal began to wane, but he kept eating the bread. He ate all along the outside of the loaf, leaving no area untouched by his mouth.

Finally, with nearly three-quarters of the loaf remaining, he put it down on the table and smiled. "That's it. I've had enough."

"Ha!" trumpeted Cierniakov. "I told you!"

"So I lost." He shrugged.

"I knew it," said the deputy. He walked back and forth in victory, telling everyone it was simply a physical impossibility. As he headed out the door, he looked at Jankel and gestured toward the remaining loaf. "You may as well keep that, too," he said.

Jankel, beaming the most contented smile, took his loaf and went and sat on his bed. The stunned silence of the barracks was shattered by an eruption of the heartiest laughter from everyone.

"So I lost!" we all echoed. "So I lost!"

And for months after that, all you needed to do to lift someone's spirits was to shrug and say, "So I lost!"

16

Khanty-Mansiysk

In the summer of 1942, as Hitler was massing his troops for the attack on Stalingrad, we at Sojma were all called to assemble in the barracks one day. No one knew why. Commandant Koltunov then walked in with a group of *nachalniks* from Khanty-Mansiysk. One of them held his arms aloft to quiet the crowd and then he addressed us.

"You were brought here under the status of Special Resettlers. That status is now ended. You are now considered refugees from Allied countries. You are still under supervision of the NKVD."

A buzz went through the crowd. We did not know what this change of status would mean. The *nachalnik* raised his arms again.

"Because the war is still on and your countries are still occupied by our common enemy, Germany, you may not, at present, go home. However, you are free to go to other places in Russia."

A gasp of joy ran through the crowd. Could it be true that we had survived Siberia? The *nachalnik* had some difficulty calming us before continuing to explain. Some regions were off-limits to us, such as the region west of the Ural Mountains and Moscow. He stressed that, since we are Allies, the best thing for us to do would be to remain at Sojma and continue the critical task of supplying wood to the Russian army in the ports of the Arctic. Certainly, we had other ideas about what the best thing might be.

He asked if there were any questions.

Salo raised his hand. "You tell us we are free, like a bird that has been in a cage for two years. And now, the cage is opened, and you are asking the bird to remain inside. Do you know of a bird that would not fly out?"

The *nachalnik* offered some verbiage in reply, but no one really listened to it. And no one stayed in Sojma.

We decided to go to Khanty-Mansiysk, where Salo was known as an excellent tailor. In fact, Salo was able to rent a house for us there. About fifty others from

Sojma also went to Khanty-Mansiysk, including the Siegal and Hochman families. Others, like Kagan and Franzel, went south to Tashkent where the weather was warmer.

As we packed our few belongings, my father saw the notebook I had been writing in, the one where I recalled my student days in Chorzow. He was afraid the NKVD would be interested to read it, so we burned it in the stove.

We bade farewell to Koltunov and Cierniakov the day before we left. They were decent men; not like jailers, but only people making the best of a situation they did not create, just like us. To our surprise, Koltunov informed my father that we had received $50 dollars in American money from my uncles Benny and Philip. The equivalent amount was given to my father in rubles.

Honoring his agreement with Hochman, who sold us the barber tools, my father paid him the other twenty-five rubles.

"Hochman," my father said. "I had no hope of receiving this. What made you make such a deal with me?"

Hochman smiled and said, "God did."

Finding Work

Khanty-Mansiysk, with a population of 10,000, was a town of wooden, two-story buildings and wooden sidewalks on the two main streets. There was a hospital, one large store called Univermag, and also a small store selling only selected food items. There was a movie theater and a dance hall. The party headquarters, the only building that was three stories high, also housed the NKVD. That building was also 250 feet long. About six kilometers away by paved highway was the port town of Samarovo, located on the river Irtish. That town had a fish processing factory.

The house that Salo had rented was located in the part of town called Perekovka. It was a log cabin, twelve by fifteen feet, with a dirt floor, heated by a fireplace oven that we could also cook with. It had two windows, two twin beds, and a table with two benches. Hassenberg lived there with us.

That first evening, we made a dinner of potato soup. We were thankful to be out of the Siberian wilderness and living in a town again, where we felt we belonged. And we felt we were an important step closer to finally going home again.

As we ate, we heard a knock on our door. The woman who had rented us the house was there, and she brought over a dish she had made especially for us, a Russian specialty called *kissel*, a type of gelatin. She waited expectantly as we all tasted it and, my God, it was the most awful thing I ever had. We just looked at each other, not knowing what to say.

"Oh my," said my father. "This is really good. Thank you very much. Gentlemen," he said, turning to us, "This ought to be enjoyed by itself. Since we've already started our soup, I think we should save this dish for tomorrow."

"Oh, yes," we unanimously concurred. The dear woman parted happy, and we were spared further exposure to the delicacy.

It was a chilly night, and we made a fire in the fireplace before we turned in to sleep. My father and Salo shared a bed, Josel and I shared the other, and Hassenberg had the warmest spot at the hearth.

I've always been a sound sleeper. I never get up in the middle of the night to use the bathroom. But, on this night, I thank God I did.

I went for the door to go out to the outhouse, and I felt very dizzy. I fell forward, almost passing out, but I reached the door and managed to open it a little. I lay in the doorway as I tried regaining my senses. My father had heard me fall. He got out of bed, and he also fell to the floor.

The damper of our stove had been left closed, and the room had filled with carbon dioxide. The fresh air had revived me.

"Salo! Josel!" I yelled.

I opened the door wide, and then went to help my father out, calling loudly to my brothers again. They both managed to crawl out themselves. I went back in and pulled Hassenberg down off the hearth. He fell like a sack of potatoes, and I dragged him outside, too. As we revived ourselves in the clean, night air, it seemed like a miracle that I ever got up. Here we had survived the winters of Siberia and almost perished by a closed damper. So ended our first day in Khanty-Mansiysk.

At first, my father and Salo worked in the homes of some *nachalniks*, but they soon opened a tailor shop. With the patronage of many *nachalniks*, they soon had so much work that they had to hire five Russian women to help.

Josel, Hassenberg, and I found work at the port in Samarovo, unloading cargo from the ships and barges. All supplies for the entire region came through these docks. They were moved to warehouses and were distributed from there. Unloading was hard work. Fifty-pound bags of flour had to be carried up a plank from the bottom of the barge and then up to the warehouse, about fifty feet away. Two people would pick up each bag and place it on your shoulder so that it leaned against your head. The trick was balancing it properly so that it did not slide off.

At first, we had to hold it with our hands to prevent it from falling. After a few days, Josel and I learned the trick of balance, which made it considerably easier to carry. Hassenberg never learned the trick. He kept dropping the bags, earning heartfelt obscenities from the men who had to help him pick the bags up again.

"You think that's bad," said Josel to the crew, jerking his thumb toward Hassenberg. "Try sawing wood with him."

Eventually Hassenberg was made one of the crew who placed the bags on the shoulders of more dexterous carriers.

The worst commodity to unload was salt. The burlap bags were only about twenty-five pounds, but the salt would come through the bag a little and rub against your skin. By the end of the day, your shoulder was rubbed raw, as if someone had taken a metal file to it.

There was a benefit to the job. Any food that spilled out of a bag was considered contaminated, and we were not allowed to put it back into the bag. But for us, this was good food, and we would stuff our pockets with it. We made sure we were not observed doing this, but the Russians must have known, and they didn't stop us. We suspected they did the same thing, too.

Josel had a great idea. He asked my father and Salo if they could make bigger and longer pockets for our work pants. Then we had pockets that reached down almost to our shoes, and we had no problem filling them. It was awkward to walk with such full pockets, but we learned to adjust.

So we ate more, and we ate better. The days of constant hunger were thankfully at an end. My father and Salo often managed to bring home delicacies like butter, meat, and fish. Since Josel and I used to come home from work earlier than Father and Salo, we did the cooking. However, the job of serving and dividing the portions went to Salo.

Whenever Josel or I complained our portion was smaller, my father had a ready answer, "The cook always tastes the food while he cooks. You guys had your share of tasting, so don't complain." He was right.

Our social life improved considerably, too. I began to attend evening adult education in the high school. I studied Russian language and accounting. Every weekend, there were theater performances, concerts, or dancing. I was already eighteen, but I didn't know how to dance. Such skills were generally not acquired in Siberia. But Salo taught me the steps of the waltz and also the tango. How odd it would have been for someone to walk into our house one evening and see Salo and me lurching back and forth across the dirt floor, humming a tango, while Josel alternately made suggestions or wisecracks.

"Salo, I'm afraid your taste in girls has been permanently damaged by the cold winters. This one is ugly, brother."

Finally my instructors deemed me ready, and we went to my first dance. At that time, we only had one good pair of pants between Josel and me, and we argued over who would wear them. My father settled it in favor of Josel because he was older. So, I had to go in my work pants with the long pockets.

I marveled at the skill of the other dancers in the darkened room and looked across the floor at a group of girls. I was too shy to move. It took quite a lot of encouragement from my brothers before I finally had the guts to walk across the floor toward a group of girls and ask one of them to dance with me. To my sheer embarrassment, she turned me down. Instead of walking back across the wide floor in defeat, I walked over to another girl who was standing alone. She said yes. I was stiff and nervous and I stepped on her foot a couple times. I apologized and explained this was my very first time dancing. She smiled. She was very nice and understanding. She helped me relax, and I tried following her lead. If not for that, I would probably never have had the nerve to dance again.

Her name was Galina Karandaszowa. I danced that night only with her. I wasn't very good, but it was fun. Galina was very friendly and after the dance I walked her home. Subsequently, we dated regularly, and she taught me some other dances.

With most of the Russian men in the army, my brothers were very popular with the girls. Salo had two girls he was very friendly with, Luba and Tamara.

Soon, thanks to my father and Salo, Josel and I got some better clothes. I even had my own necktie. We brothers preferred to wear the European-style shirts and jackets while my father favored the Russian *rubaszka*, which was basically a long shirt worn over the pants.

After a few months, we moved from the house in Perekovka to a room we rented in a house located much closer to the center of the town. The house had one big room and also a large kitchen. The landlady rented us the room, which had two beds, and she slept with her two children in the kitchen. Hassenberg found another family to live with. The advantage of this was that the landlady frequently cooked meals for us. She was delighted to do this because we managed to bring home food she could not possibly get and we shared it with her. I remember occasionally Salo bringing home what looked like a very lean bird and even though it did not have much meat, it gave a better taste to the potato soup we ate daily.

Tamara, Salo's girlfriend, used to come to our house, and she sometimes brought along some fish. She cooked a fish soup the Russians called *ucha*. That was the first time we were introduced to that dish. My brothers and father liked it very much, but I must admit, as indiscriminate as I was about food, I did not particularly like *ucha*.

Though no longer driven by hunger, Josel and I still used to spend our leisure time arguing about the time we could go home and what dish we would ask our mother to cook first. Now we expanded the discussion to what we would do if we caught Hitler, Goebbels, or any of the other big Nazis. Just killing would be too good for them. Josel favored frying them in a large frying pan. I preferred treating their open wounds with salt.

At first, while we were in Khanty-Mansiysk, we looked down at the Russians and thought we were more intelligent and better educated than they were. That changed gradually as we got to know them better and saw they were no different than us. In many instances, we admired them for their ingenuity in adapting to hardship and adversity. We were also united with most Russians in our fear of the NKVD. They treated everybody—Russian, Jew, or refugee—the same way.

In the winter, when the Irtish was frozen, we worked in the warehouses and also made deliveries to nearby settlements by horse-drawn sled. Occasionally Josel and I would work in the print shop, turning the huge, steel wheel of the printing press. Whenever there was some problem with the electrical power, we were asked to help operate the machine manually. It was really hard work, but it paid well and it was different, so Josel and I did not mind.

The following spring, I was assigned to work on the river tugboat that pulled the barges. We made a number of trips to Tobolsk, a few hundred kilometers to the south. We picked up supplies, and I worked loading. Josel was assigned to the barge. On the way, the captain showed me how to operate the tugboat. After a few trips, he allowed me to take the wheel and steer. I even learned how to dock.

One day after we returned from a trip, I went home, but Josel decided to remain on the barge to clean up and get it ready for the next day's trip. By the time I got home, Salo and my father told me that the barge Josel was on had broken loose and floated away down the river.

We all ran to the dock and sure enough, the barge was gone. The tugboat captain was waiting for us, and we boarded to look for Josel's barge along with a second tug. We went down all the way to where the Irtish flows in to the Ob River, but we saw no sign of him. One of the passing boats coming up the Ob told us they had not seen any barge either. We were really worried. Even if the barge broke up, we would have had to see its debris. We turned back upriver.

This time, each of the two tugboats went close to each side of the riverbank. The captain explained he had to be very careful to stay in deep water. To prevent us running aground, I stood at the bow, testing the depth with a long pole. That time of the year, the river was overflowing, flooding into the marshes and swamps. The grass in the marshes was very high. It was possible the barge had floated into one of these high grass fields.

So we started to shout into the marshes, and sure enough after a while we heard Josel call back. But we couldn't see him or the barge. We put a small rowboat over the side. A crewman rowed, and I went with him. There nestled in the grasses, was the barge, perfectly intact. Josel sat cross legged smoking a cigarette, as if he was waiting for the trolley in Chorzow.

"Josel! Are you all right?"

"Sure," he said. "Why not?" As he climbed down into the boat, he calmly said, "I knew you were going to find me."

We all envied Josel and his schmoy-boy attitude, even though none of us could understand how he could be so calm in this kind of situation. I probably would have been scared to death.

In fact, about a month after that, I was scared to death.

We had completed building a new barge, and we were ready to launch it into the river. The barge was built on the riverbank where the ground sloped down to the water. One side of the barge was resting on the ground at the top of the slope. The majority of the hull was supported by wooden pilings, which made it level with the top of the slope.

To launch the barge, long logs, at least two feet in diameter, were placed on the ground immediately below the barge and extending all the way to the water. The bark was stripped, and grease was applied to the top to make a slippery ramp. The idea was to use long rods to knock out some of the support pilings, causing the elevated side of the barge to drop down onto the greased logs and slide into the river.

To make it easier to knock out the support pilings, a crew crawled underneath to cut a notch in every second piling to weaken them. This crew consisted of Josel, me, and a few Russians.

I was cutting these notches, unaware that the rest of the crew had finished and gotten out from the bottom of the barge. I became aware of this in a horrible instant when I heard, like a gunshot, the cracking of wood as some of the notched pilings began to give under the weight of the barge above me.

Everyone began to shout, "Get out, Simon! Quick!"

I began crawling frantically, and I heard more cracking. I didn't think I had enough time, so I pressed myself to the ground next to one of the greased logs. That way, I thought, if the barge falls, it will slide down right above me.

Fortunately for me, the cracking stopped, and I quickly scrambled out to safety. I was breathing heavily. I looked at Josel. He was white, and there was no trace of schmoy-boy in his expression.

I stepped back as the crew used the rods to knock down the weakened pilings, as planned. The great barge fell with a splintering crash and slid down like a rocket. The hull made a thunderous clap against the water and sent a broad arch of spray out toward the middle of the river.

That's when I noticed that the greased logs had, by the weight of the barge, been pressed completely down into the soft ground of the riverbank until they were all but buried. If I had stayed there, I would have been crushed into the thickness of a sheet of paper. I felt dizzy and weak in the knees realizing how close I was to death. Josel, of course, had regained his composure completely.

"Well, you don't look too good," he said, putting a hand on my shoulder. "But you look a lot better than you would if you had stayed under there."

"Yes." I smiled weakly.

I knew that Josel and I had just performed our last job notching pilings. Why any of the Russians, who knew the danger, ever volunteered for it is beyond me.

Late that evening, the family went to sleep, but I was restless. I guess I was still dwelling on my close call. I went outside to sit in the street in front of the house. I noticed in the sky the unearthly vast colors of the Aurora Borealis. As I gazed upward, Josel came out, too. He came to see how I was, but he stared upward too and didn't say a word. We were overwhelmed and speechless, as if hypnotized. I had survived today. But if I had died, this unspeakably beautiful phenomenon would still be spreading itself across the entire sky. The glory of the measureless universe is significant. The people who might look up to see it occasionally are comparatively insignificant.

When Passover came, the Siegal family invited us to their Seder. We all helped them bake matzo. About twenty people were at the Seder dinner. About half had been at Sojma. There was much conversation, and some of it was about the Communist government. One man, Abramson, was very critical and even cursed Stalin.

About a week later, Abramson was arrested, and we never heard from him again. His wife kept on inquiring at the NKVD. At first, she was told he was being interrogated. Later, they said he had been transferred to another district where anticommunists were kept. We knew that such a "district" would not be a comfortable place.

Someone at the Seder must have squealed. A few weeks later, one of them, a man named Green, suddenly left Khanty-Mansiysk. We heard he moved to

Omsk. We only could assume it was he. They probably interrogated Green, and he succumbed to their threats and implicated Abramson.

In 1943, we learned a Polish general was organizing a Polish exile army to fight the Germans. Immergluck corresponded with some offices in Moscow and received information that the nearest recruiting center was in Omsk. He spoke to the NKVD and was told that anyone who wanted to enlist could travel to Omsk.

Josel persuaded my father to let him go. He was twenty-six. Salo was thirty-five, and I was nineteen. Josel and a group of about fifteen other young men went to Omsk, but they returned a few days later. The recruitment office had filled their quota, and it was closed.

We heard about the victory in Stalingrad and the Russian troops advancing and taking back the Ukraine. In September 1944, we were advised that, within a week or two, we would be transferred closer to Poland to the territories already liberated by the Russian army. We welcomed that news, even though we didn't know exactly where we were going. And we didn't know that, a month earlier, the last Jewish ghetto in Poland, in Lodz, was liquidated. 60,000 Jews were sent to Auschwitz. They followed closely behind Anne Frank and her family, who were sent to Auschwitz from Amsterdam. We only knew this: we were taking another step closer to home, and the Germans were retreating from Russia.

With our imminent departure from Khanty-Mansiysk, Salo told my father he wanted to marry Tamara. We all liked her very much. It was almost like she was a part of our family already. Tamara's parents approved, too.

But we were not sure the NKVD would allow a Russian citizen to travel away with us. Salo checked with the authorities and was advised that if they marry officially, she would be able to go. Salo hurriedly arranged to get a marriage license and the last day before we left, we had a wedding dinner at the home of Tamara's parents.

It was a bittersweet evening for them. They liked Salo, and were glad to see their daughter happy. But they also knew they would probably never see her again. They had already sent three sons to the army, and didn't know what their fate might be. Only Tamara's younger sister remained home with them. As we finished our meal, then had cake, we tried to keep the conversation light. Tamara's mother smiled and had tears in her eyes. I marveled at how tough a decision Tamara had to make, but she seemed confident, sure, and happy. I wondered if I would ever know love such as that.

The modest wedding of Salo and Tamara reminded me of the only other sibling whose wedding I had attended—Lisa. I marveled at how different her wedding was.

Lisa Eichel

Lisa was born in Piotrkow in 1906, my father's first child with his first wife. Lisa was his only daughter. She was about fifteen when her mother died, and she stepped into the role of homemaker and even advisor to my father. She was always self-assured, and she had poise beyond her years.

After she completed *gymnasium*, she helped my father in the store. In fact, she pretty much ran the day-to-day operation of it, doing all the bookkeeping and interacting with the authorities. She also personally handled the important and wealthy customers. She was always my father's favorite, and he respected her immensely.

She was also respected among her friends, all rich, German Gentiles. They were a dashing crowd. One of her friends, Lizi Kutner, even flew an airplane, something that only very few could afford. Even among them, Lisa distinguished herself as glamorous. The cost of her wardrobe exceeded the combined cost of everyone else's in the household.

She had many suitors, and she turned her nose up at all of them.

My father used to say, "Lisa would like to marry a handsome, rich, Jewish doctor or lawyer. But there are none in Chorzow. And, if there were, I couldn't afford the wedding anyway."

My father should have added that Lisa would only marry a German, handsome, rich, Jewish doctor or lawyer. She was completely assimilated in that culture, and would not even look at the many newcomers from Poland who were flooding the city.

It was inevitable, when my mother joined the family, that there would be clashes between her and Lisa, each jealous of the other's influence over my father. One big one came when Lisa told my father she wanted to buy a tennis racquet and learn to play. (She already had tennis outfits because it was stylish.) Tennis at that time was distinguished as the sport of the very, very wealthy, so, of course, most of her friends played. Racquets were very expensive.

My mother objected fervently. She said we could not afford such a luxury at a time when we were breaking our heads daily on how to pay our bills. Business was not that good. She was probably right in her arguments, and her vehemence was undoubtedly fueled by resentment at Lisa's squandering of family resources. Of course, Lisa got her tennis racquet, though she never learned to play.

By the time Lisa was twenty-four, she still had no serious boyfriend in sight. My father actively started to look for someone. In addition to Lisa's list of criteria, he added one more. He wanted someone who was connected to the men's clothing business. He had told Lisa he planned to give her the store as a wedding gift.

Once, he took her along on a business trip to the city of Lodz. She was then introduced to a very charming son of a wealthy textile manufacturer named Miszliborski. They were in the city for a few days, and Lisa spent most of her time with that young man. Before they left, the young man told my father he liked Lisa very much and that she had promised to write to him.

On the way back, my father asked, "Well? What did you think of him?"

"He seems like a fine young man," she said. "Look what he gave me." She showed my father a diamond ring.

My father was delighted beyond words. To please Lisa was hard enough, but also to have a son-in-law in textile manufacturing? He could not dream for anything better than that.

When they came home from the trip, he waited until she was in her room and then quietly reported, "I think this is the right man for Lisa. I think she likes him, too."

Later that evening, he asked Lisa to show the ring to my mother and Salo.

"I sent it back to him with a note," she said calmly. "I told him I'm sorry, but I cannot accept such a gift.

"What!" my father exploded. "Sent it back? How did you do that?"

"I put it in an envelope and mailed it."

"You mailed it?" he yelled. "You put it in an envelope—such an expensive ring—and dropped it in a mailbox? Are you out of your mind?"

She shrugged.

"He was a very nice young man," my father wailed. "You said so! He could give you an excellent future! He could be a great help to our family! And you put a diamond ring in an envelope and mail it? Are you crazy?"

The incident gave him sleepless nights and left him feeling helpless.

Not long after that, Jicryk Russ, the oldest brother of my mother, came to visit us from his home in Bendzin, near Sosnowiec. Jicryk was a jovial man who had a piece goods business, and he entertained at weddings by telling stories and singing. He knew everyone in town. My father occasionally had business in Bendzin and sometimes he would take us along to visit Jicryk's family. My father was considered their rich uncle.

On this recent visit, Jicryk told my parents he had the right person for Lisa. He was the younger brother of one of the very well-known men's clothing wholesalers in Sosnowiec. His name was Alex Wrona. My father knew of the Wrona business in Sosnowiec; however, he doubted Lisa would be willing to talk to anyone from that city.

Uncle Jicryk was persistent. "Why don't we try it? The worst thing that can happen is nothing."

My parents agreed it could not hurt to try. They concocted a plan. My father took Lisa along on his next business trip. On the way back, as usual, they had to change trains in Katowice. There was a layover before the connecting train to Chorzow. He took Lisa to the Cafeteria Turecka at the station for coffee. It was a place she liked to go.

As they entered the cafeteria, they spotted Uncle Jicryk "by accident" with a young man. Jicryk immediately jumped up from his table and greeted my father and Lisa with great surprise, insisting they join him at his table. Then he introduced his friend, Alex Wrona, who bowed and kissed Lisa's hand and held out a chair for her to sit down. She was charmed by the attentions and elegant looks of this new gentleman.

Soon Alex and Lisa were engaged in small talk and hardly noticed when my father and Jicryk excused themselves and left the table on some thin pretext.

When they returned, it was time to go to the train.

"Mr. Eichel," Alex asked, "would it be permissible with you, sir, if Lisa took the next train after this one? I will make certain she doesn't miss it."

My father fully expected Lisa to decline. But, to his surprise, she did not. Of course, he granted permission. Jicryk walked him to the train platform, and they agreed to get in touch with each other as soon as they got a report from Alex and Lisa.

We were surprised that evening when my father came home without Lisa.

"He's an excellent young man," my father said of Alex. "He's very elegant and well-spoken. She seems to like him, too. But that could all change fast when she finds out he's from Sosnowiec. Who knows?"

Lisa finally arrived home at eleven o'clock. Everyone was anxiously waiting for her. She was very cheerful and gay when she walked in. It was not the same Lisa. We silently watched her smiling, doing graceful dance steps from room to room, humming a melody, and not bossing anyone around or demanding anything. She teased us for a long while by saying nothing.

Then she coolly told us, "Mr. Alex Wrona is an exceptionally interesting young man." She smoothed her hair. "He asked me for another date." She looked at our expectant faces and made a mock frown as if to fool us. "I told him yes."

The next day after Lisa went to the store, Moniek and I went into Lisa's room and looked around, hoping to see what kind of a gift she got. She always used to bring home some kind of a gift from her dates. We looked all over, but didn't find anything, though we did notice a chocolate bar on her dresser. We thought maybe my mother accidentally left it there. We split half of the chocolate bar between ourselves and left the rest with the wrapping on the dresser.

In the evening when Lisa came home, she went into her room. A moment later, we heard a piercing scream. We all rushed in. Lisa stood in front of the chest with both hands on her face. She was sobbing.

"Who took my chocolate?" We couldn't comprehend how the chocolate could be linked with the scream.

"Chocolate? What about it?" my father asked in disbelief.

"I got this from Alex," Lisa murmured, gently cradling the remaining chocolate.

"We took it," I stammered. "Moniek and I. We didn't know it was yours."

She glared at me. If looks could kill, I would have perished on the spot.

"What? You thought it was Josel's maybe? On my dresser?"

We filed out of the room, my father shaking his head in disbelief. "A diamond ring…she sends back in an envelope. A cheap bar of chocolate…she screams like murder."

When he came to dinner not long after, we treated it like a High Holiday. We dressed in our best, and my mother set an elegant table. Alex arrived wearing a very stylish fur coat. He was as tall as my father was. He had dark hair and a "Douglas Fairbanks" mustache. In no time, he was easily conversing with everyone. He made an excellent impression. My parents and even Salo liked him right from the start.

Later she went to dinner with his family and after that he visited us frequently. It became clear they were well-suited to each other. Uncle Jicryk arranged for my parents to meet Alex's family and discuss wedding arrangements.

Around that time, a monumental argument was going on between my mother, my father, and Lisa. Even though my father had promised Lisa the store as part of her trousseau, my mother insisted she would retain the pants section of it. She personally always took care of that section. My father said this was such a small amount of business that it was not even worth discussion. However, my mother was insistent. She felt it was important to have some income in addition to the tailor shop. She prevailed, but it only after a lot of loud arguments.

After the meeting of the parents of the bride and groom, the wedding arrangements were made. A little over a year after they first met, the religious wedding was held in Bendzin. If we did it in Chorzow, my father said, we would have to invite half the city. Alex's parents said the same about Sosnowiec. Only close family on both sides was invited. This amounted to 150 people. There was an orchestra and a *batchin*, a kind of master of ceremonies, who entertained between the musical programs. I guess, in a way, it was a last hurrah for us in our life before the war. By contrast, Salo and Tamara's wedding was modest and quiet, but it was very loving all the same.

Lisa and Alex settled in their own apartment in Chrozow. It was set up partially from gifts they received and partly from things taken from our house, including all the linen and towels.

My mother said, "Lisa took from our apartment everything that wasn't nailed down."

By contrast, Salo and Tamara easily fit everything they owned into a single suitcase.

17

Barvenkovo

We booked passage away from Khanty-Mansiysk on the last boat leaving Samarovo. The river had already begun to freeze. We managed to reserve a small, private cabin for Salo and Tamara's honeymoon suite. They had spent the night at her parent's house, and they were late arriving at the boat. The captain was impatient, and we had to pay him to delay the departure a little. I was frantic with worry, but my father and Josel calmly stared in toward shore. Finally, about fifteen minutes late, they arrived, hurrying toward the dock. Salo held their suitcase, and Tamara bravely clung to his arm as they came aboard.

The boat took us to Omsk, where we boarded the Trans-Siberian Railroad. We were accommodated once again in a freight car, this time with as many as forty in our car. The train was packed with refugees from all over Siberia. Though it was cramped and uncomfortable, we all felt freer. We were heading closer to home.

The trip was interminable. I don't know how many days we traveled. When we reached the Ukraine, the train made some stops. We saw groups leaving the train and boarding trucks that took them into the nearest town.

When we reached the town of Barvenkovo, our car door was pulled open and we all got out, stiff-legged, blinking in the sunlight of our new place.

A bit larger in population than Khanty-Mansiysk, Barvenkovo is located a few hundred kilometers from the Ukraine city of Kharkov. It was relatively easy to rent a room since most of the families had their men away in the army and were eager to earn extra income by renting. Salo and Tamara rented two rooms in a house. One was to be used for tailoring. We were able to rent a room in another house, and, once again, the woman was pleased to cook for us.

Josel found a job delivering supplies and picking up produce from some outlying villages. Before we left Khanty-Mansiysk I had completed my course in accounting, so I had no problem getting a clerical job in the office of the Kharkowskaja Torgovlia, which controlled the distribution of food and supplies to all retail stores in the region. My first assignment was the control of rationed goods like bread and other foods. Each person received coupons for his or her allotment that were turned in at the store at the time of purchase. My job was to make sure that each store accounted for their sold products with the appropriate number of coupons. With the wartime shortage of so many items, I had to keep records using the margins of the *Pravda* newspaper. We just didn't have enough blank paper. A pen or pencil was hard to get, so you had to be really careful not to lose it.

I soon came to understand that my position carried with it some degree of power. When I bought bread for myself in the store, paying for it and using my ration coupon, the store manager herself would personally take care of me. She would smile as she weighed my portion, which was always a generous one. In return, I found a way of casually letting her know in advance if we had scheduled a spot inspection of her store.

"I understand that tomorrow in the afternoon is supposed to be fine weather." She understood what that meant.

I was the only man in an office of six women. It was my task to deliver our reports once a month to the main office in Kharkov. When I first learned of this assignment, I was very happy since it would give me an opportunity to see the city of Kharkov with all expenses paid. Little did I know of the problems the journey would present.

Even though there was a train station in Barvenkovo, the only scheduled trains in wartime that went in the direction of Kharkov were only going to local towns, then back to Barvenkovo. I had to first go to Lozowaja, which was about 100 kilometers in the wrong direction, and required a change of trains, or hopping a truck. Once I made it to Lozowaja, I had to somehow get on what was always an oversold train to Kharkov.

If that wasn't hard enough, my travel voucher covered only the expense of the direct, prewar fare from Barvenkovo to Kharkov. Here I was, on official government business, yet I had to somehow circumvent the system just to get my job done.

On my first trip, I was lucky. I learned that an express train from Moscow to the Crimea, which was passing through Barvenkovo, would be stopping at Kharkov. I had also noticed through trains usually slowed down as they passed through Barvenkovo station. I managed to jump on to this train.

But, of course, I had no ticket. The train car had individual compartments, so I just stood in the corridor. When I saw the conductor entering the car, I ducked into the bathroom to avoid him.

At one point, a woman in her midtwenties passed and we struck up a conversation. I could tell by her clothing that she was a city girl. I learned she was from Moscow and was working for the government. She had been awarded a vacation trip to the Crimea.

She could see I was not Russian, and she was anxious to learn about life outside the Soviet Union. I enjoyed talking with her until I saw the conductor enter at the far end of the car.

"Excuse me," I said. "I have to go now."

She grabbed my hand. "You don't have a ticket?"

I reluctantly admitted the truth and gently tried to free my hand. However, she squeezed tightly, led me to her compartment, and drew me inside. He mother was seated there, and we exchanged greetings as I gratefully sat down. I explained, even though I was on official business, there were problems with transportation. They were not surprised.

"It's not any different in Moscow," the mother said. "Unless you pay off someone, you can't get anything."

I enjoyed riding with them all the way to Kharkov.

The Kharkov train station was intact, but the city had been heavily bombed. A great number of buildings had taken direct hits, and they were in complete ruin. However, there were several undamaged, modern high-rise buildings. The streets were wide and remarkably clean. Trolley cars and buses were operating, so it was relatively easy to get to anyplace within the city. My pulse quickened again, being back in a city.

I had no problem finding the Kharkowskaja Torgovla office. There were about forty employees, mostly women. I was told I would have to take back some papers and reports that would be ready the following day. They arranged a place for me to sleep over.

On the return trip, I managed to get a ticket to Lozowaja easily enough. But the train was way oversold, and I had to stand the whole way. In Lozowaja, I jumped onto an express train that was passing through Barvenkovo. It too was full. I managed to duck the conductor until we were practically approaching Barvenkovo. I gave him a sob story and a few Russian cigarettes and that took care of the problem. I trusted the train would slow down in Barvenkovo, so I didn't break my neck jumping off. But luck was with me, and the train stopped there to take on water.

I made this roundabout trip every month without any serious problems. I always carried the currency of cigarettes and sometimes even vodka. I was soon to learn how strong that currency really was.

The director of the Barvenkovo region of the Kharkowskaja Torgovla was a war veteran we called Nikita. His hand had been paralyzed in the battle for Stalingrad. A very likable person, he was around thirty years old. Like most Russians, he enjoyed his drink. He was always very jolly and joked with everybody. I was never sure whether this was his nature or his beverage.

Once, when I was at the office in Kharkov, I had just turned to leave when Nikita walked in and boomed out, "Simon! My lad, how are you? Listen, I'm glad to see you."

He explained he was there to pick up supplies in a truck, and he asked me to help him. Though his manner was jovial, he was my boss, and his request was really a command. But I was happy to help him and also happy to have a ride all the way back to Barvenkovo without having to crisscross the Ukraine as usual.

I followed him to the warehouse side of the building and helped stack the merchandise on the loading dock. He then asked me to stay and watch it while he sauntered off to get the truck. By the way he spoke, I assumed it must be parked somewhere around the corner.

But after an hour he still had not come back and I began to worry. The office and warehouse were already closed. All of the merchandise was sitting there, and I was responsible for it. It was getting dark. I had no idea what to do. I paced back and forth and strained my ears for the sound of a truck engine.

Finally I heard it. It grew louder until a big, American Studebaker truck rounded the corner. A soldier was driving it, and the ever-buoyant Nikita sat next to him. It was all I could do to restrain myself from blurting out, "My God! Where the hell were you?"

The soldier and I then packed the truck. To my surprise, the soldier waved and walked away. Nikita said he would return in the morning and we would drive back to Barvenkovo.

"In the meantime…" he said, motioning me to the back of the truck.

He opened a box and took out two cans of beans.

"Damaged in transit," he said.

I didn't know what he was talking about. The cans look undamaged to me. For a guy with only one good hand, he worked very nimbly and didn't need help. He opened them with his knife and dumped the contents into a couple plates he produced from somewhere in the back of the truck.

"Ah, Simon." He smiled. "We live like czars!" Then he pried the plug off a barrel of vodka. "Give me a hand here, like a good fellow." He held his empty bean can near the hole as I tilted the barrel. He filled both our cans.

I was dumbstruck. This was definitely against regulations.

"We have a reservation this evening at the Hotel Studebaker." He motioned me toward the cab of the truck. As we settled in, he toasted to my health, took a long pull from his drink, and dug in to his dinner. I sat still. I was confused. Technically, we were stealing. Could Nikita be giving me some kind of a test?

No, I thought, he wasn't that kind. And anyway, he was busy plowing through his own dinner. I was hungry too.

"Drink!" he said, taking another gulp.

I began eating the beans, but I did not touch the vodka.

"Come on, man, drink. By God, will you?"

I took a small sip.

"There you go. It'll be cold tonight. You don't want to freeze. Have some more."

I think I must have done just that because the next thing I remember it was daytime and the truck was bouncing down the road, and my head hurt like hell. Nikita sat unperturbed between the driver and me. We were already outside the city.

An hour later, we stopped in front of a *stolovaja*. Nikita took half a pail of vodka inside, and he put it on the counter next to the woman at the cash register.

"Good morning to you, madame," he said. "I have here good vodka. I need a good meal for my two comrades and me." The woman dipped a fingertip into the vodka and then touched it on her tongue.

She smiled. "Please sit down, sir."

Again I was dumbfounded. To be so open and public about it, even though it was plainly illegal, was something I could not comprehend. There were quite a few people in the place and obviously many saw and heard everything, but nobody reacted. We enjoyed a complete meal with potato soup, a plate of chicken and kasha, and hot tea with bread and butter. Nikita chatted amiably as we ate, but I could only wonder what would happen when we got back to Barvenkovo and the shortages were discovered.

We made two more stops before we got back, and the same scene was repeated each time. I must admit I ate more than I usually eat at home, but none of Nikita's frequent entreaties could get me to touch the vodka again. I was astounded by how much he and the soldier consumed; like it was spring water. But they never appeared to be drunk, and the soldier did a fine job driving. On the last stop, I saw the soldier helping Nikita pour water into the vodka barrels.

Fortunately, it was late evening when we arrived back in Barvenkovo. I thought the late hour would make it easier for us to unload without any scrutiny. As we pulled up to the warehouse, I saw, to my complete horror, the leader of the

Communist party and the chief of police waiting for us with the warehouse manager. I had an impulse to throw open the door of the moving truck, jump out and run away. I almost had a heart attack. But Nikita and the soldier were as calm as they could be.

I tried to act nonchalant as we unloaded the truck, but any minute I expected to be arrested and carted straight back to Siberia. Instead, I saw Nikita and the warehouse manager fill two large containers with vodka. They gave one each to the leader of the Communist party and the chief of police. They also put some canned goods into bags for them, and they left. It was as easy as that, and all the time I was worried sick. The warehouse manager did not even bother to check the shipment.

I went home and breathlessly told my father what happened. When I finished, he looked me straight in the eye.

"Don't you dare tell this to anyone. Ever. You saw nothing. Forget about it."

I could refrain from talking, certainly, but I could not forget about it. I understood they compensated for the stolen vodka by simply pouring water into the barrels. But how could they account for the missing cans of food?

I knew the woman who handled the control of the warehouse. She was very friendly with the warehouse manager, but up until now I don't think she suspected anything. I expected trouble after she reviewed the last shipment, but she found everything to be in order. I wondered how this could be, but I didn't dare ask her about it. Later on, I found out there was a write-off of items "damaged in transit," which the warehouse manager signed. So that was what Nikita meant.

Most of the people we socialized with in Khanty-Mansiysk were now in Barvenkovo too, so our social life picked up where we had left off. We went to movies, theater, and dances. I began to date a girl about my age who, coincidentally, was also named Galina, just like my girlfriend in Khanty-Mansiysk. My brothers had fun with that.

"You fall for any girl at all, as long as her name is Galina."

My new Galina had served in the army and was wounded in the leg, leaving her with a slight limp. She was good-looking and a little shy. Josel's girlfriend was named Viera. We usually went out together on double dates.

In March 1945, Edward, son of Tamara and Salo, was born. I became an uncle again. I wondered how big Felix, Lisa's son, would be the next time I saw him. The day Edward was born, Tamara's increasing labor pains sent Josel and me running to the hospital to get the doctor. By the time we came back with the doctor, Edward was already crying. The woman living in the next house helped deliver him. His first crib was the drawer of the dresser pulled out halfway and stuffed with soft blankets.

This was at a time of increasing optimism as news of the war had, for some time, been one German loss after another. We knew it was only a question of time. Then, in May it was over. The joy overflowed everywhere. We hugged each other, cried, and embraced all our friends for days afterward.

We thought we could go directly home, but, in Soviet Russia, it wasn't as easy as that. If you wanted to travel, you had to have a passport. Being without it, we were still under the supervision of the NKVD. When we inquired, we were obligingly told, yes, we could acquire a passport if we accepted Soviet citizenship. Of course, we declined this. We wanted to go back to Poland. My father had written a number of letters to his brothers in America, but we had not received any reply. We didn't know if they even got our letters.

There was a discussion in Salo's apartment attended by Marcus Immergluck and some of the other refugees. They felt there was a possibility the Polish government that was now being formed may not know we were here. Our families didn't know. It was decided to send a delegation to Kharkov, where we heard there was a Polish committee. Marcus Immerglick and Salo were chosen to go. They carried a good supply of vodka and cigarettes with them.

The trip was worthwhile. In August, a few months after they returned, we boarded a special refugee train going back to Poland.

18

The Return

It was August 15. In the Ukrainian city of Barvenkovo we stood on a threshold: my father, Josel, Salo and Tamara and Edward, six months old, and Hassenberg. It had been six years since we were torn away from home. The very air we breathed that day in Barvenkovo was more intoxicating than the best Russian vodka. In our minds, we were already walking the familiar streets of Chorzow. It had been a German city when we were driven out, but it was a Polish city now.

We packed our few bags. Everything we had, my father, Josel and I fit into two medium-sized suitcases.

"We came with nothing," said my father, "and we are going home with practically nothing."

A light rain fell in the grey streets outside, but it could not dampen our spirits.

"We're going home!" yelled Josel, waving his hands and dancing around in the room in a ballet of joy.

My father could even feel the elation pulsing like an electric current between us. His eyes shone with it.

"Simon!" blurted Josel. "What's the first thing you'll do when you get home?"

How many times over the years did my big brother ask me this question to lift my spirits and distract me from hunger?

"I will hug my mother and Moniek," I said, "so hard they will never forget it."

My father nodded. "They won't forget."

"How about you?" I asked Josel.

I thought he would concoct an elaborate meal that my mother should cook with meat and fish together. Instead he looked at my father as if making a request.

"I want to have a dinner with the whole family, like we used to have on holidays. Mother, Lisa, Alex, Felix, Moniek, Salo, Tamara, Edward, you, Simon, and me." His face beamed as he visualized it.

"We'll need to extend our dining room table." My father smiled. He turned to me. "When you left, you were just a kid. You are returning as a man. I wonder if your mother will recognize you."

"I wonder," Josel interjected, "if we will recognize Moniek? He's seventeen now."

"I will never forgive myself," my father shook his head, "for not giving him a little *letzgelt* when we left." It was not the first time he said this in the last six years. Each time, lines of regret cut into his face.

"You'll give it when you come home this time," said Josel. "It will be the best ever."

"What about Felix?" I said of my nephew. "He's eleven now."

Our happy chatter continued as we left our room and walked to Salo's apartment. That night, we all slept there.

Hassenberg came over early the next morning and we went to the Barvenkovo train station, as full of anticipation as can be.

The excited crowd was contained by a number of policemen led by an NKVD officer. Grouped tightly together, we passed through the police checkpoint, where he checked our names off a list. Another police officer led us to the train.

Unfortunately, we were taken to a freight car again. We had hoped for better on this triumphant journey. But it was understandable, with such a flood of refugees on the move. And they put only about twenty people in each car.

"At least we have room to stretch out on the floor," Josel said. "The gestapo was not so accommodating."

Soon the whistle blew loud, and the train lurched forward and began to roll. "*Es soll sein mit mazel* (It should be with luck)," called my father aloud.

"We're on the way," shouted Josel. Edward, startled by the train whistle, had begun crying. His doting parents smiled and soothed him.

We stopped in the city of Kharkov, where they added additional cars to the train. Then we turned west. The train stopped at least three times a day, usually near a city railroad station. There were always tables outside where some Russians handed out food and drinks. Occasionally we had some tea and at least once a day, we got hot soup. There were also peddlers selling bread, milk, and sometimes fruits. We were not hungry.

I don't remember how many days we traveled. It all blends together when you're in a boxcar and can't really see the scenery. But we rolled out of Russia and into eastern Poland. At every stop now, people were disembarking. It seemed impossible to understand; we were really back in Poland again! Our own country.

At all the stops in Poland, groups of local people gathered to see the trains arrive. They would ask where we were from and where we were going. There was a conspicuous absence of any Jews.

But at one station, there was a solitary Jewish man who asked us where we were from. We replied and asked him the same.

"Tarnogrod," he said, naming a city we already passed through. We asked him if he found his family.

"*Farbrent* (burned)," he said and sadly walked away. We didn't understand why he would say that.

We left the refugee train in the city of Katowice. There, we boarded a commuter train to the city of Chorzow.

Home

One would think, of all the experiences in my life that I remember, this most desired time would be recalled most clearly. But it's not so. One would think that at the very least I would remember with clarity the details of our first arrival. But I don't. I have absolutely no recollection of that day.

I'm shocked that this is so. And I guess shock is really the right word. We, all of us, must have been in a state of shock. What else could explain it?

We found no one from our family: my mother, Moniek, Lisa, Alex, or Felix. No one to hug so hard they would never forget it.

Our apartment was occupied by a communist official's family. They came soon after the Russians occupied our city. They knew nothing about the people who lived there before. They would not even invite us in.

Our store was now being operated by the state. I don't remember what was there or how it looked.

We found no one from Uncle Yankel's family: Yankel, his wife Rachel, his sons Izik, Mendel, and Karl. Their apartment was occupied by a Polish family who knew nothing about the people who lived there before.

Hassenberg found no one from his family: his wife Gucia, and daughters Regina and Mia. His apartment too was occupied by a Polish family who knew nothing about the people who lived there before.

For the first few days, we found not a soul that we knew, Gentile or Jew. I guess it was more than my mind could grasp; the streets and buildings so familiar, but no one here but strangers, as if we had been away a thousand years.

Then we chanced to meet Mr. Taub, who used to be a member of the Jewish committee in our city. We met him in the building of the Jewish public school I used to attend, which was now converted into a public kitchen and shelter. I believe we spent one or two nights there. The people there were all Jews in search of family, like us. Each desperately asked anyone for the smallest clue that could help him or her find loved ones. We learned nothing.

Mr. Taub was a survivor of Auschwitz. He was the first to tell us about the concentration camps.

No such news had reached us in Russia. I'm not sure the information really reached us when we heard it from Mr. Taub. How could it be possible? How could it happen? Why?

He told us no one from his family had survived. He did not know anything about our family. We were sorry for his loss. But surely our family could not have perished. Perhaps they were in Sosnowiec.

We went there and found no Jews. No Jews in Sosnowiec? How could it happen? The only answer we got was they probably went to Auschwitz.

The same happened in Bendzin. We found no one from the Warszawsky family, my aunt, and the Russ family, my uncle, or anyone of Alex Wrona's six brothers and their families.

We stayed for a time in Chorzow in a two-room apartment somewhere on Ulica Wolnosci. I don't recall where Hassenberg stayed. My father wrote a letter to America telling them where we were, and that we were looking for our family, and asking them if they knew anything. We felt, if anyone survived somewhere, they would probably write to America, like we did from Russia.

A few weeks later, we received a postcard from Uncle Philip in New York. It was written in Yiddish. It said "Forget the dead. Go to the American zone in Germany, and we will try to bring you to America."

Gone

On that small piece of cardboard, with so few words scrawled on it, the inevitable truth came crashing down on us like an ax. All the evidence we had seen around us in the past few days became focused on the blade of the ax. It severed our weak hope. Everyone from our family was dead.

The strength that sustained us through war and winter; gone. My mother was gone. My father held the postcard in limp fingers. Moniek was gone. My father's eyes filled with tears. Lisa, Alex, Felix. Gone.

My heart wanted to cry, but my eyes had only salt and no tears. An ache worse than hunger spread through my chest and my stomach. All I could see was the awful confirmation in the pain on the face of my father. All I could say to myself, "No. No. No."

19

America

We all agreed that to stay in Chorzow was tantamount to living in a cemetery. But, to get to the American zone in Germany, we would have to cross borders illegally. That would be tough enough, but having little Edward made it even tougher.

But there was another, more immediate problem. I was twenty-one years old, and eligible to be drafted into the Polish army. If I were to leave the country after receiving notice from the army, I would be a deserter. That notice could come any day. If we wanted to go anywhere at all, I had to go immediately.

We learned about an underground branch of the Hagana, the Zionist military organization that later became the Israeli army. The underground branch, called the Brecha, smuggled people to Israel via Austria and West Germany. They were particularly looking for young people. All I had to do was spread the word that I wanted to go to Israel. The best place to do that was in the public kitchen. I did this.

The following day, as I sat drinking tea in the public kitchen, a man I didn't know sat down across from me, a little to the side.

"Do you want to go to Israel?" he asked, sipping his tea, but not looking at me, just staring blankly ahead.

"Yes," I said. "I want to go."

"Be ready tomorrow morning, eight o'clock sharp," he said, still not looking at me. "Take the trolley from Rynek to Bytom. Carry only a small bag." He got up and walked out.

At home, I told my father. He immediately got hold of Salo and Josel to discuss the situation. They all still thought of me as the kid. They weren't comfortable with me going on my own for the first time and thought maybe Josel should go with me. But this was rejected. Josel would be needed when my father, Salo, Tamara, and the baby had to go.

"I'm not a kid," I said to my father. "You said so yourself."

Still, I left the decision to him. He wrestled with it, but eventually decided that I should go. As soon as I got to Germany I was to send a telegram to America so they would know where I was. My father immediately wrote a letter to his sister, Rifka Mayerowitz in America, explaining the situation.

I was given some money and a carton of cigarettes. I packed a few clothes and a couple of sandwiches and I was on my way early the next morning to the Rynek station. Before, I had felt confident that I could do it, but now, walking on my own to the station, I felt vulnerable.

I arrived on the platform about fifteen minutes before eight. While waiting, doubts plagued me. What would happen if the trolley car came a few minutes early? Or late? How would I know which one to take? And once I boarded it, where should I get off in Bytom? The man never told me. I couldn't even say if I'd recognize him again.

Just as I heard the sound of the trolley approaching, someone tapped me on the shoulder. A man pointed to the oncoming trolley car and said, "That's your car."

Before I could turn around, he walked away.

I boarded the trolley car and sat down, still filled with anxiety because I didn't know where to get off. A few stops later, just as the door opened, a man passing me said, "Get off here." He stepped out of the car.

I hurriedly grabbed my bag and stepped out a little behind him. He pointed to a man wearing a white cap who was walking about fifteen meters ahead.

"Follow the man in the white cap, but keep a distance."

Before I could absorb what he said, he walked away in the opposite direction. I started to follow the man in the white cap. After a few blocks, he suddenly stepped into the doorway of an apartment building. By the time I got to the building and entered, the corridor was empty. But a door opened, and someone motioned me inside.

I entered the apartment and, to my amazement, saw Marek Lichtblau among the handful of people in the room. Marek was a classmate of mine in the Jewish public school. He had arrived in the apartment a half hour earlier, using the same cloak-and-dagger process I did. He had survived Auschwitz, lost his entire family, and decided to go to Israel. He did not know anything about my family, but he confirmed a great number of people died in the gas chambers of Auschwitz.

In the evening, we were taken to the railroad station and boarded a train to Wroclaw. There we got off and were told to follow each other about ten or fifteen meters apart. At one point, we were approaching a police station and for a minute, I thought something had gone wrong. But, not far past the police station, we went through a large gate into a yard surrounded by three-story apartment buildings. There were some big trucks in the yard, and we noticed people lined up and boarding them.

There were hundreds of people around. We were taken to a room on the top floor of one of the buildings. We were given some sandwiches and hot tea and were told to rest and not leave the room.

In the middle of the night, we went down into the yard where we climbed into one of the trucks. Marek and I made sure we stayed together. There were three trucks in our convoy, going in the direction of the Czech border. At one point our truck was stopped by two Polish soldiers and we were told to get out. One soldier, who obviously was bought off, explained that there was an inspection at the border station and that we would have to walk across the border undetected. He walked with us for a while, and then pointed in the direction of the border, and left us. We proceeded across the border, where we met a Czech army patrol. They in turn took us to a nearby Red Cross shelter. There we got some hot food and sleep.

In the morning, we boarded some trucks and were driven to Bratislava. Here, too we were in a complex of apartment buildings surrounding a large yard. The walls of the yard had scribbled names of people that had been here. I added my name, hoping to leave a trail for my father and brothers, should they pass this way. Most of the people there were Jewish.

The next morning, we assembled in the yard.

A man spoke to us. "You will march through the city to the railroad station. Officially, you are Greek refugees heading home. Do not speak Polish. Do not speak German."

We were lined up in rows of four. Those in the first row carried a red, communist flag. By now, more than 100 men and women were in our group. People on the streets asked us where we were from. We just shook our heads, as if we didn't understand. Some were very persistent, so Marek, who was marching next to me, answered in Hebrew, "*Ani me jodaja* (I don't know)." Then he whispered to me, "They don't understand anyway."

We boarded a train for Vienna. The station there was in the Russian zone, and we were reminded again not to speak Polish or German. We marched through the city to the Rothschild Hotel in the American zone.

We were greatly relieved to reach the American zone, and I saw my first American soldiers. We stayed overnight at the Rothschild Hotel and in the morning we boarded another convoy of big trucks. A few hours later, we arrived in a refugee transit camp in Linz, Austria.

Linz was a crossroads. Those who wanted to go to Israel were moved to a different section of the camp. There was no one there from the organization that helped me out of Poland to be sure I went on to Israel. I simply bid farewell to Marek Lichtblau and went to the German section of the camp. I assume Marek ended up in Israel.

The following day, we boarded a passenger train and went to Ulm, Germany. At the German border, some American soldiers got on the train. One of them accidentally dropped his rifle.

"Shit," he cursed.

This word, the first I ever heard in English, was translated for me by one of the people sitting nearby.

Mary

We were taken by truck to the Sedan Kaserne refugee camp, which was formerly a German army camp. Now it was called a displaced persons (DP) camp. When we got out of the truck, we saw groups of men, some of them American, wearing the uniform of the United Nations Relief and Rehabilitation Administration (UNRRA). They lined us up and determined who among us spoke English. A handful of Hungarians responded. They were enlisted to help translate what the officers told us.

We all were dusted with DDT to kill lice and given a blanket, a towel, soap, and an ID card. We were also assigned a bunk. I was assigned to one of the large rooms with fifteen or more beds in Building A. Eight, large buildings, housing about 2,000 displaced persons, were numbered A through H.

Another building housed offices, the kitchens, and dining rooms where we had three meals a day. The food was pretty good.

The camp occupied the entire city block on Sedan Street. An iron fence surrounded the camp with the entrance guarded by the camp police. These police were appointed from the DP population.

To leave the camp, you needed a pass from the camp office. Nearly all of the people who worked in the office were English-speaking Hungarian refugees who had arrived on the same transport as me. The previous transport of refugees from Poland had vacated the camp to make room for us.

There were very few passes issued. The first time I tried to get one, I was turned down. Right after that, I saw a Hungarian man about my age who was given a pass. I approached him.

We had a difficult time communicating. He spoke only Hungarian, though by trial and error, I learned that he also understood a little Yiddish. So, I was able to explain to him that I spoke German and could be helpful to him outside the camp. He understood and secured a pass for me with no problem.

We went to the post office, and I sent a telegram to my Aunt Rifka in New York. As we walked back to the camp, we passed a house with a little garden in front. A man was picking apples from his tree. I took out a cigarette and held it up so the man could see it.

In German, I called to him, "Can we have an apple? I have cigarettes."

The man picked up the basket that was half-full with apples. He walked over to us with an amazed look on his face. I thought he was going to reprimand me for making so poor of an offer. Instead, he put down the basket in front of us, snatched the cigarette from my hand, and ran into the house shouting, "Marta! I have a cigarette!"

We stood there for a long moment, not sure what to do. Then we emptied the basket. We put the apples into our pockets and walked away. Each of us ate a sweet, fresh apple. We got more than a dozen apples for one cigarette.

As we walked back into the camp, we were holding some apples in our hand. Within a minute, a crowd had surrounded us, offering German marks for the apples. Within ten minutes, we sold all the apples and had a handful of marks. So, in addition to making a cash profit, that one cigarette gave enjoyment and nourishment to more than a dozen people.

I told my partner, "If you supply the passes, I'll supply the cigarettes."

In the next few days, we made three or four more trips. All were equally successful.

Then I was called into the camp supervisor's office. The supervisor was a Dane named Van Eyk who spoke to me in German. "You cannot sell apples or anything else in this camp. That is black market trading and is strictly forbidden."

I thought I might be arrested, and felt I had to offer some defense.

"I can't live on what I get in charity from the kitchen," I said. "I don't want to be in the black market, but I need to work. But it seems there are no jobs available in the camp."

Instead of jail, I was referred to the camp's welfare officer, Mr. Thomas. He was a black, American officer, about thirty years old, six feet tall with a welcoming disposition. He seemed to smile when he spoke. He had a young, Christian, Polish woman as his secretary and translator. At first, she spoke German with me, but she then switched to Polish when she found out I came from there.

I again explained to him that I would like to work, that I spoke Polish, German, and Russian and I had experience in accounting. I left his office being told that there were no jobs available. Soon after that I got friendly with his secretary. In subsequent conversations, she promised to see what she could do.

I asked for some notebooks and pens, and they were given to me. I began writing my story down again, just as I had in Sojma.

Not long after that, I was called into the secretary's office and she told me I had a job in the camp warehouse. The warehouse was a large room on the same floor as the offices with cartons of clothing, notepads, pens and pencils, and many other items. The manager was a Polish Christian, and I replaced his assistant, who had been transferred to another camp. Our job was to distribute goods to the camp population based on lists provided to us by the welfare office. At least once a week, we received shipments from various charitable organizations.

Only a week later, the manager was transferred to another camp and I became the warehouse manager. The first shipment I received had a number of canisters of Hershey chocolate bars. When I opened the cans to check how many bars were inside, I found a number of them had been broken into small pieces. I had not seen or eaten any chocolate since the war started, and all broken chocolate was fair game. I ate so much chocolate that, after a day or two, I could not even look at it anymore.

I needed someone to assist me in the warehouse, and it was left to me to choose that person. I found very little in common with the Polish Jews in the camp since most of them came from small towns in Poland. The Hungarians were more educated, city people that I could identify with. However, most of them spoke only Hungarian. As I was pondering who to select, we had an incident in the camp.

At night, someone outside the camp threw a stone into one of the open windows of Building A. It hit a girl in the head. The girl, one of two sisters, was bleeding, but she was fortunately not hurt badly. The whole camp talked about this. At the time, I did not know the sisters personally, but I certainly had seen them. They walked around in the camp wearing short shorts, and they looked extremely sexy.

The younger one, Edith, who had been hurt, was about seventeen years old and her sister Lizi was a few years older. They were Hungarian, though Lizi spoke a little German. I asked her if she wanted to work with me in the warehouse, and she gladly accepted. Though the camp committee and the Hungarian man running the offices had both put forth other recommendations to me, they didn't complain when I hired Lizi.

Shortly after the incident, Lizi and Edith moved into an apartment on Sedan Street where two of her cousins lived. A few days later, she invited me to a dinner in her apartment, a meal she cooked herself. That was the first time I had Hungarian cuisine.

She served some noodle soup and when I took the first spoonful, it was very, very spicy. I thought that maybe she did it as a joke, so, when she happened to get up from the table, I switched my plate of soup with hers. I waited until she came back, sat down, and took the first spoonful of soup. I watched her expression. Sure enough, she looked quizzical. Then, to my amazement, she picked up the paprika container and added more spice to her soup. Edith had observed me switching plates, and she now told Lizi. I explained that I was on to her joke. She burst out laughing, saying she had purposely put less spice in my soup. We all had a good laugh. And so I learned that Hungarian food is quite spicy.

The first thing I did as the manager of the warehouse was to take a complete inventory of everything we had. I gave the completed list to Officer Thomas, who was astonished at all of the things we had there.

"I had no idea we had some of these things," he said. I found shoes, caps, sewing needles, yarn, and many other items he was not aware of. I also posted item inventory cards on all bins. Once a month, I provided an inventory to the welfare office.

Around that time, I became friendly with a Hungarian guy who worked in the kitchen. Joe always gave me large portions. He was nineteen and had a sister, Mary, who was four years older. Through Joe, I became friendly with other Hungarians, some of whom spoke German. However, whenever I was with a group of them, they always lapsed into Hungarian even though they also knew German. I had to constantly remind them I was there, too. So I started learning Hungarian and soon gained passable control of it.

One day, Joe asked me if I wanted to live with him and his sister since they had an extra bed in their room. I gladly agreed. There was no privacy sleeping in a large room with fifteen other people. Joe and his sister lived in one of the three-room apartments in the camp on the second floor of Building H. The apartment also had a small kitchen. Our room had three beds, a table with four chairs, some cabinets, and chest of drawers that we shared. For me, it was a welcome change.

What I did not know at that time was that Joe had an ulterior motive. He wanted me to get to know his sister. But, when I first met Mary, she spoke only Hungarian and was not particularly kind to me. She did not particularly like Polish or German Jews, me included. I liked her though.

One day, I met Mary on Sedan Street and, as we walked, I tried to get a little too friendly for her liking. She slugged me in the pit of my stomach, a punch so hard that I doubled over and struggled for breath for a few minutes. I quickly learned to treat her with great respect.

One of my jobs as warehouse manager was providing blankets, soap, and other items to new arrivals. I was part of the welcoming party. Whenever a truck pulled in with new arrivals, as I handed out the blankets, I would ask, "Is there anyone here from Chorzow?"

One day, one of the men on the truck, an older man, said he was from Chorzow and asked me who I was. I told him. He looked at me and said "I know the Eichels from Chorzow, but I don't know you."

It turned out he knew my parents well. After all, I was only a kid before the war, and he would not know me. To my delight, he told me that he met my father, Salo with his wife and child, and Josel in the Vienna railroad station, but he did not know where they were going. That was about two weeks prior. I was thrilled to realize they had made it out of Poland. They must be somewhere in Austria or Germany, but where? I went to Officer Thomas and told him about my family being in Vienna two weeks ago and asked if he could help me find them.

His secretary translated his sarcastic reply. "Oh sure, Simon. It's no problem. After all, there are only about a thousand displaced persons camps in Germany and Austria. It won't be hard to find them at all."

"If you help me find them, I'll give you a whole bottle of whiskey." I promised. I knew he could get everything at the army PX, except whiskey.

"You have a deal." He instructed his secretary to start calling each camp first thing tomorrow morning.

Only two days later, the secretary informed me that in one camp, they confirmed that there was an Abram, Alexander (Salo), and Josef Eichel registered. But it was five o'clock and the office was closing, so they couldn't call them to the phone. She promised she would call this camp again tomorrow morning first thing at nine o'clock. My heart soared.

The next day, I went to the warehouse an hour early to get some work done so I could go to the phone at nine o'clock. As I was working, somebody came knocking at the locked warehouse door. I was upset since we usually opened the warehouse for distribution at ten o'clock.

I kept on shouting, "The warehouse is closed! Come back at ten o'clock."

But the knocking persisted and grew louder. I got mad. Cursing, I stormed to the door and flung it open. To my amazement there stood Salo. Tears were streaming down his face.

"You little *Scheisser* (shitter)!" He smiled. "We've been looking for you all over Germany!"

We hugged, and I pulled him inside. He looked like hell; pale and soaked to the skin. He told me that yesterday evening the office in his camp in Hofgeismar gave him a message that I was looking for them. He immediately went to the train to go to Ulm. He had to ride on the roof most of the night, and it was raining. He was coughing. I usually did not cry, but this time I couldn't hold back tears of happiness.

My father had told him to bring me back to their camp, but, seeing I had one of the most prestigious jobs in the camp, Salo thought it made more sense for them to come here. We called my father. After some discussion, he agreed.

The following day, Salo went back to Hofgeismar to prepare to come to Ulm. Meanwhile, I found a bottle of whiskey for Mr. Thomas.

Hope Is Unbroken

At that time, it was customary for people to announce names of survivors whenever large groups of people were assembled to help people find their relatives. One of the guys from our camp was going to a wedding in Zalsheim. I asked him to announce my name there.

The following day, I went to see a German boxing match in the nearby sports hall. At one point, I stood up from my seat, shouting encouragement to one of the boxers. Someone tapped me on the shoulder. At first, I thought the person sitting behind me wanted me to sit down and stop blocking his view.

As I sat, I heard the person behind me say, "Siegfried, Siegfried."

In the camp, I was known as Simon. I whirled around. At first, I did not recognize the man who called me Siegfried.

He looked at me for a moment. "I'm David Warszawski," he said. "Your cousin!" We embraced awkwardly across the row of seats.

"Come on," I motioned to him. "Let's get out of here."

We went to a nearby café for tea as David told his story. One year older than I, he was the son of Yicryk and Yocheta, my mother's sister. They had lived in Sosnowiec. David explained he had attended the wedding in Zalsheim. More than a few people there were announcing names. It was noisy and difficult to hear.

David did not hear my name announced, but he overheard a man next to him telling a woman, "Siegfried Eichel is alive! I am going to find out where he is."

The man moved off through the crowd to find the one who announced my name.

David approached the woman. "Did he say Siegfried Eichel?"

The woman turned out to be my Aunt Sophie Chencinski and the man was her son Richard, who had been such a strong influence on me in my days at *gymnasium*.

I nearly wept as David continued.

Sophie knew David's parents in Sosnowiec, but didn't know the children personally. David didn't know the Chencinskis. At the wedding, they pieced it together, and he and Richard realized they both were my cousins.

The morning after the wedding, David left for Ulm to look for me. When he got to the Sedan Kaserne, he spoke to the police chief. I was friendly with the chief, and he knew I had gone to the boxing match.

Of course, I was overjoyed to hear that Richard and his mother were alive. But this joy and the joy that arose from our finding each other faded fast. David confirmed my mother, Moniek, Lisa, her husband Alex, and their child Felix had all perished in Auschwitz. David also told me that his entire family, except his younger brother Abramek, had perished in Auschwitz, too.

David himself had recently married an Auschwitz survivor. They, with his brother, lived in the Zalsheim DP camp. We finished our tea and left the café.

"Siegfried," he said. "Next week is the first night of Passover. Come to our Seder."

"Thank you. I will come."

"I'll contact your family in Hofgeismar and invite all of them, too." Tears were in his eyes. He took off his wristwatch and pressed it into my hand. "Please," he said. "To remember this day."

Not only did David invite my family, he arranged for their transportation from Hofgeismar. At David's Seder in Zalsheim, I was reunited again with my father, Josel, Salo, Tamara, and Edward. We also embraced Sophie and Richard there.

Again, there was bitterness amid the joy. Sophie confirmed my Uncle Yankel, his wife, three of their four sons, his daughter Gucia (Hassenberg's wife), and her two daughters had all perished in Auschwitz. She did not know about Yankel's oldest son, Max. But she was sure all our relatives in Piotrkow had also perished. Richard's older brother, Izik, had survived and now lived in Sweden.

We all stayed in Zalsheim that night and the following day, all went to Ulm. I had managed to reserve only one room in a house on Sedan Street. It was very tight quarters for four adults and a child. However, after a few weeks, they moved into a two-room apartment with access to cooking facilities on the same floor. By then, I was staying with Joe and Mary in Building H.

Josel did some haircutting in the camp, but later teamed up with someone driving a truck. They were licensed to go to the nearby farms and buy milk to sell in the camps.

Salo got a job in the camp's employment office as an assistant to the American officer in charge. Before long he was practically running the office. Later, he was one of only three displaced persons who were ever promoted to Class Two UNRRA officers, the highest rank for a DP employee. He was given an UNRRA uniform and had full access to the United States Army PX. He also was allocated an apartment in a building on Hassler Street outside the camp.

Meanwhile, we applied for emigration to the United States, but we were not hopeful. We learned that the Polish quota had a long waiting list and, on top of that, those who were in West Germany in 1945 were considered first. I arrived in 1946.

Orphaned children up to the age of fifteen were given top priority. There were very few of these in our camp. But, because none of the DPs had birth certificates, some who looked young managed to pass for being fifteen. They were the first to go to America. Mary's brother, Joe, tried, but he was turned down. He was nineteen and looked it. We had no other choice but to wait.

One day, a man came in to the warehouse and asked if I was Eichel. He handed me a photograph and told me my cousin Max Eichel asked him to give it to me. It was a picture of Max with the following note, handwritten in Yiddish, on the back:

> *Nisz gebrochen is der gloiben es kimt doch der sheine herlicher friemorgen der sztam boim Eichel der iz da zol und vet veiter sein der fackel fun den hois di hevra mindel di bekerin.*

This means, "Hope is unbroken that there will come a beautiful free morning when the Eichel family tree will continue to be the torch from the house of Mindel the Baker." Our grandmother Mindel was known as Mindel the Baker.

The man told me Max's story. In 1938, a group of five young men and a woman, some of them our relatives from Piotrkow, came to Chorzow and asked my father if he knew someone who could help them cross the border, into Germany, illegally. They intended to wind up in France. Max volunteered to help them cross the German border and go with them all the way to France. A few days after they left, three of the men returned. They had been arrested in Germany and sent back to Chorzow. Max and the others though, made it to Paris. Max was now living in Belgium.

New York

I had been doing a good job in managing the camp warehouse. I was promoted to managing the regional warehouse located near the Boelke Kaserne, about ten blocks away from the camp.

As part of the promotion, I attended a two-week management course the UNRRA gave in a facility in Nellingen, West Germany. This is where we stayed for the duration of the course. We had professors from Harvard and Heidelberg Universities. The American and German approaches to the subject differed substantially, which sometimes caused confusion. The American professors stressed the importance of supervision and motivation of employees. The Germans stressed the importance of planning and discipline in execution. Despite this confusion, I enjoyed the class very much.

We were given numerous writing assignments. In one of them, we were asked to describe how we would restructure and manage our present workplace. At the end of the course, we received a diploma stating we had successfully completed the UNRRA management seminar.

A week or two after I returned to Ulm, I was called into the regional supervisor's office. To my great surprise, a high-ranking American army officer who I had not seen before was seated in the office with the supervisor. I thought he was from the military police. I was really scared and tried figuring out what I had done to warrant police involvement.

I sighed with relief when he was introduced to me as the area supervisor of the United States Army Supply Division. He spoke to me in German and said he had read my written report on reorganizing the regional warehouses, and he would like me to do it.

To say that I was surprised would be a gross understatement. I was shocked. After all, I had treated the subject only as a school assignment. One of my suggestions was to take products currently stored in a single warehouse and divide them across the entire five-warehouse system to avoid bottlenecks and improve distribution. But I was currently managing only one warehouse.

I mutely turned these thoughts over in my mind, but the supply officer was a man of few words. Before I had a chance to ask any questions, he turned to our regional supervisor and stated I was now in charge of all the warehouses. Both shook my hand, congratulating me and wishing me luck on my new assignment. I walked out of the office in a state of shock and worry. I struggled to remember the details of what I had written in the seminar. I didn't have a copy of it.

Within a month, I had reorganized the warehouses, and my system was fully operational. It proved to work well. Six months later, they promoted me again. This time, I became the sub-area commodity accountant. I reported directly to the area chief of property and commodity accounts in Stuttgart.

For this new position, I was required to inspect all camp warehouses in our sub-area, which included ten camps with Jewish populations and also the Estonian camp in Göppingen. It required a lot of traveling, so I was assigned a Jeep with a driver for each trip.

By the end of 1947, relatively few people had passed all the emigration requirements and had been granted entry to America. Among those who did make it were Lizi and Edith. It seemed there was practically no hope for emigration to America, even for people who had relatives there, like us.

There was still active recruitment of young people for illegal transport to Israel. Josel and I would have been able to go easily. However, my father, Salo, Tamara, and Edward would have to apply for legal emigration to Israel. The low annual quota for that made it unlikely they would ever get there. So Israel was eliminated from consideration.

By this time, I was seriously dating Mary. My father took me aside one day and laid down the rules.

"If you want to fool around with a German girl, I don't care," he said, looking me in the eye. "But don't fool around with a Jewish girl, understand? Are you serious about Mary?"

"I am, Father."

"Does she know this?"

"Not yet."

"Let her know, or else stop spending so much time with her. It's not right."

The next day, I spoke to Mary and told her my intentions. As I expected, she told me she felt the same way. (In our time together, I had given her no further cause to haul off and punch me.)

Today, young people decide to marry on their own, but it was not that way for us in 1947. We then had to take the next step of asking permission of our parents, just as Salo and Tamara had done and all the generations before.

But Mary's parents were not alive. Her father died before the war, and her mother perished in Auschwitz. Besides Joe, she also had an older brother, Ferry, who lived in the DP camp in Leipheim. My father felt, in the absence of parents, he wanted to talk with Ferry. So my father, Mary, and Joe went to Leipheim by train and spoke to Ferry. At the end of that conversation, Mary and I were officially engaged.

The wedding was on June 27, 1948, in our apartment on Sedan Street in Ulm. The *chuppah* was in the courtyard, and the reception was in the apartment. We had about forty people. Salo and his family had just moved to their new apartment on Hassler Street, so Mary and I moved into the room they vacated.

Shortly after that, we learned that applications for emigration to Australia were being accepted. We decided that, if we could all be together, we should go there. The difficulties in getting to America showed no sign of easing.

The plan was that Josel and Joe would go first and we would follow after we heard from them. We heard Australia's German quota was better than the Hungarian one. Josel had papers made that stated he was born in Germany. We decided that Joe, who had a tougher chance, would register first and Josel would register one week later. The idea was, by the time Josel's papers were processed, we would know if Joe had passed.

Joe did pass, but he had to leave for Australia before Josel got his answer. Two days after Joe left, Josel received notice that the German quota was filled! Our strategy had failed, and it was a real tragedy. Joe was already in transit, and there was no way to stop him. A week later, we got a card from him that was posted from Naples, Italy, where he was boarding a ship to go on to Australia. Mary, my poor wife, cried her heart out. We might never see Joe again.

The good news of 1948 was that, after 2,000 years, Israel was now an independent Jewish country. This increased the hope we might all be able to go there legally. Ferry went there.

Another good development came at the end of the year. The American consul in Stuttgart was replaced by one that was much more favorable to Jewish applicants. Even though we still had to play the quota game, it was now much easier. Because the Hungarian quota was better than the Polish one, we decided Mary would be the primary applicant and I would go along as her husband. She had an aunt in New York, and they sent her the appropriate sponsorship papers. Our application was granted. In August 1949, we boarded a ship for New York City in the United States.

The day before we left, my father gave me $7 (American).

"We've all heard that in America, gold grows on the street and all you have to do is bend over and pick it up," he said. "I haven't been there, but I refuse to believe there is a country in this world where you don't have to work for a living. So be prepared for it. I have not seen my brothers and sister for a long time, but, if they are poor, they will not be able to help you. If they are rich, then they probably worked very hard for it and are not about to give it away to you. So don't expect it. And, when you talk to my brothers and sister, give them the same respect you give me."

Epilogue

Mary and I arrived in New York City on August 15, 1949. We came in to Pier 23 in Manhattan. My uncles Benny and Phillip and his daughter Mildred met us there and took us to Uncle Philip's apartment in Rego Park, Queens. Philip's wife, Kathy, greeted us warmly at the door and showed us to the room they had made ready for us. They called it the "Refugee Room" because all relatives who came to the United States stayed there first.

A couple of weeks later, I got my first job; a stockman at Times Square Stores in Ozone Park, Queens. (It was later called TSS Department Stores.) I earned $30 for a workweek of forty-four hours. I also went to night school to learn English.

In October, Mary got a job as a seamstress in my cousin Singer's tailor shop. She earned $40 for a forty-hour workweek. That gave us enough to rent a room in an apartment on Lot Avenue in Brooklyn.

Soon after we vacated the Refugee Room, new tenants arrived: Father and Josel. Father got a job in the same tailor shop where Mary worked. Josel worked in a barbershop in Queens.

Early in 1950, we learned Salo, Tamara, and Edward would be coming soon. We moved to a three-room apartment on East 28th Street in Brooklyn that we shared with my father and Josel. At the same time, we reserved a similar apartment in the same building for Salo's family. By that time, I had also received the first of many promotions at TSS. I became a salesman with a $5 increase in salary plus commissions. The following year, Salo got the same position with a TSS store in Brooklyn.

Josel married in 1952. He and his bride Molly moved into an apartment in Richmond Hill, Queens. The following year, their son Harold was born.

We got word that Hassenberg had settled in Israel. Every year for the rest of his life, Josel and I sent him a check for $25. The first one had a note attached that read, "For the bread we took from you in Sojma."

There followed a fruitful period for our family. All my father ever wanted was to work and to take care of his family. Now, in America, we could do it. We found no gold lying in the streets, but we did find opportunity. That we were not American born, that we could claim no station in society, that we were Jewish, that we were refugees—none of it mattered. We had just as much opportunity as anyone else.

In 1954, Mary gave birth to our daughter, Margaret. After that, Mary quit her job. I was by then an assistant store manager and was transferred to Bay Ridge, Brooklyn—the highest-volume store in the chain. Also that year, Salo's second son, Robert, was born. The following year, Josel's second child, Jeffery, was born. In 1956, our second daughter, Evelyn, was born.

The 1960s began on a dreadful note. My father died. It was a terrible shock to me. I couldn't stay in the apartment where he died. I was a store manager now, and I could afford a house. We bought our first new house in Laurelton, Queens. Around that same time, Josel and a partner bought their own barbershop.

I had a series of important promotions in the 1970s and ended the decade as a vice president and director of merchandising for the TSS chain. It was a long way from the warehouses of the displaced persons camp system in Germany. Even longer from the days of peddling stockings on the black market in Lvov. In 1976, my daughter Margaret, a speech pathologist, married Dr. David Liu.

In 1980, Salo retired and bought a condominium in Florida, a long way from the icy winters of Siberia. I retired in 1987, but that condition proved to be short-lived. The following year, Mary's cousin, Peter Galambos, founded a wholesale distributorship of medical supplies called Medi-Source. He asked me to come in as director of operations, which I did. I was glad to help. That was also the year that my daughter Evelyn, a PhD in psychology, married Charles Rogers, a vice president at Pepsico. Their daughter Jessica was born in 1990.

Josel was a heavy smoker all his adult life and it got the better of him in 1992 when he died of lung cancer. Two years later, Margaret adopted a daughter, Erica. The year after that, Evelyn's second child, Nicole, was born.

Peter sold Medi-Source in 1997. I retired again, this time (I thought) for good. But, Evelyn founded E. Rogers Associates, Inc., a human resource management consulting firm, later that year. In her judgment, I was bored, so she hired me as CFO. I was able to negotiate the privilege of working from home.

In 1998, Margaret adopted a second daughter, Sara. Mary and I celebrated our fiftieth wedding anniversary. We sold our house in Bellmore, Long Island, and moved to a senior citizen community in Westchester County. During the packing for that move, I found the two notebooks that gave rise to this memoir.

The following year brought the death of Molly, Josel's widow, from emphysema. In 2001, Salo died at the age of ninety-three. In 2004, I celebrated my eightieth birthday.

Auschwitz has become a museum to unspeakable cruelty. The record of horrors committed there remains an open wound on the flesh of our species.

Mary and I have seen our lifetime as parents and how quickly it has passed. Our daughters have grown, and their daughters seem to be growing up even faster. And I want their children and grandchildren to know this story. I hope they never have hardship, but, if they do, I hope the echo of this story comes to their ears. Value your family. Never lose hope.

978-0-595-36136-6
0-595-36136-6

Printed in the United States
48072LVS00003B/379-411

9 780595 361366